Praise for *Curveball*

"It takes a lot of courage to stand on a pitching mound trying to live up to the worth of a paycheck. But what it takes to openly share the transformation from a man with such self-loathing to a man with the most authentic self-love is profound. I have the utmost respect for this man who is breaking boundaries and disrupting the status quo."

—MATTHEW MORRISON, ACTOR, DANCER, AND SINGER-SONGWRITER

"Everyone knows what an amazing pitcher and teammate Barry Zito was, but *Curveball* gives readers a glimpse into the personal highs and lows and family dynamics that Barry experienced, beginning as a child. As baseball players, we dream of getting called up to the big leagues, but things aren't always as glamorous as they seem. We can all learn something about the importance of our God-given purpose, perspective, and relationships from *Curveball*. Barry uses his life experiences, both good and bad, to show us that who we are and how we treat people are much more important than any 'superstar' label we may wear. This is a book that I'll be sharing with many people, young and old, both in and out of the game of baseball."

—TIM HUDSON, FORMER TEAMMATE, MAJOR LEAGUE
BASEBALL PITCHER, AND WORLD SERIES CHAMPION

"Here is a must-read for everyone who dreams of making it big! Barry's conviction, courage of self-reflection, and relentless search for meaning takes us on a path through material success to self-discovery in a higher power. A compelling memoir that entertains and reveals with every page!"

—BOB ROTH, CHIEF EXECUTIVE OFFICER, DAVID LYNCH FOUNDATION

"Being fortunate enough to experience many of the highs of a baseball player, I can relate to a lot of Barry's stories. What I can relate to the most is the false promise that money and fame will fulfill the eternal longing we have for peace and happiness. Only through God's grace have I been able to find that sense of being that I longed for."

—BUSTER POSEY, FORMER TEAMMATE, MAJOR LEAGUE BASEBALL
CATCHER, AND THREE-TIME WORLD SERIES CHAMPION

"A gritty, nail-biting, edge-of-seat yet heart-opening experience. Whether you believe in God or not, you will believe in a higher order that drives our individual and collective actions toward our greatest purpose and potential on earth. Barry Zito shows us that we can go from prove-aholic to full alignment within ourselves if we put our true spirits on the line."

—MIKI AGRAWAL, FOUNDER OF THINX, TUSHY, AND WILD AND AUTHOR OF BESTSELLERS *DO COOL SH*T* AND *DISRUPT-HER*

"Occasionally you meet someone and are struck by their genuine kindness and affability. Barry Zito is that someone. His generous spirit, humility, and presence are both a gift and a shining example of what it truly means to be a human being. Barry's story is one of struggle, giftedness, honesty, and redemption. You will be inspired to greatness and reminded that hope always outlasts suffering."

—JAMIE GEORGE, LEAD PASTOR, JOURNEY CHURCH, NASHVILLE, TN

"This book made me smile, it made me laugh, it made me sad, and it even made me cry. More than anything, it made me proud of my teammate and friend! Having spent so much time with Barry, I [knew] many of the stories covered in the book but never realized the inner struggle. Barry outlines beautifully how God worked through him and helped him along the way throughout his career and life. Amazing read from an amazing man with an amazing family!"

—MARK MULDER, FORMER TEAMMATE, MAJOR LEAGUE BASEBALL PITCHER, AND WORLD SERIES CHAMPION

"Barry Zito's book is a scathingly honest look at his own life. He takes us inside the highs and lows of his journey through baseball and the subsequent life of celebrity and excess that ensued. Throughout it all, Barry looked for answers from every possible source, searching for success on the mound and fulfillment in the deepest reaches of his soul. None of these philosophies, traditions, or lifestyles ended up sustaining him. His then soon-to-be wife, Amber, introduced him to Christianity. We are witness to the incredibly transformative power that giving his life to Christ brought him. The power of letting God work through him. This is a baseball story with a curveball, that what we think we need is not really that at all. That grace can permeate all the twists and turns of our lives, leading us to our true purpose. An inspiring story!"

—MIRA SORVINO, ACADEMY AWARD-WINNING ACTRESS

CURVEBALL

CURVEBALL

How I Discovered
True Fulfillment
After Chasing
Fortune and Fame

BARRY ZITO

WITH ROBERT NOLAND

W PUBLISHING GROUP

AN IMPRINT OF THOMAS NELSON

Published in Nashville, Tennessee, by W Publishing, an imprint of Thomas Nelson.

Photo insert design by Rachel Hampton.

Thomas Nelson titles may be purchased in bulk for educational, business, fundraising, or sales promotional use. For information, please e-mail SpecialMarkets@ ThomasNelson.com.

Unless otherwise noted, Scripture quotations are taken from the Holy Bible, New International Version®, NIV®. Copyright © 1973, 1978, 1984, 2011 by Biblica, Inc.® Used by permission of Zondervan. All rights reserved worldwide. www. Zondervan.com. The "NIV" and "New International Version" are trademarks registered in the United States Patent and Trademark Office by Biblica, Inc.®

Scripture quotations marked MSG are from *The Message.* Copyright © by Eugene H. Peterson 1993, 1994, 1995, 1996, 2000, 2001, 2002. Used by permission of NavPress. All rights reserved. Represented by Tyndale House Publishers, Inc.

Scripture quotations marked NLT are from the Holy Bible, New Living Translation. © 1996, 2004, 2007, 2013, 2015 by Tyndale House Foundation. Used by permission of Tyndale House Publishers, Inc., Carol Stream, Illinois 60188. All rights reserved.

The names and identifying details of some individuals have been changed to protect their privacy.

Any Internet addresses, phone numbers, or company or product information printed in this book are offered as a resource and are not intended in any way to be or to imply an endorsement by Thomas Nelson, nor does Thomas Nelson vouch for the existence, content, or services of these sites, phone numbers, companies, or products beyond the life of this book.

ISBN 978-0-7852-2788-5 (eBook)
ISBN 978-0-7852-3086-1 (Special Edition)
ISBN 978-0-7852-3330-5 (Special Edition)

Library of Congress Control Number: 2019901083
ISBN 978-0-7852-2766-3

Printed in the United States of America
19 20 21 22 23 LSC 10 9 8 7 6 5 4 3 2 1

To my wife, Amber, for inspiring me to shine every bit of the light God gave me. I am honored to share a loving home, a beautiful family, and a God-centered life with you.
To my mom and dad. I miss you and love you both.
To my sisters, for being there for me all those years.
To my manager, Robert Filhart. Without your belief in me, this book would have never been written.
And to God, for loving me in spite of myself.

Contents

CONTENTS

Foreword

by Billy Beane

In over thirty years in the Oakland Athletics front office, I've seen more than a thousand players come through the clubhouse at the Coliseum, and many more travel throughout the A's farm system. Some players come and go without my getting to know a lot about them beyond their performance on the field. Other players I actually do get the chance to know. We talk about baseball and the world beyond baseball, I meet their families, and I socialize with them outside the confines of the ballpark.

But there are only a handful of players over the last three decades who stand out the way Barry Zito does.

From the moment that Barry walked into the clubhouse, a mere thirteen months after being selected ninth overall out of USC, it was clear that he was different. And not just in the way that most left-handed pitchers are different from the rest of the population. Barry was thoughtful and outgoing and generous and curious, all in a way that belied his youth and his complete lack of big league experience. Back then, none of us knew the story that you're going to read in the pages to come. What we knew was that this self-assured, good-looking, Southern California kid with a lights-out curveball could potentially be the perfect complement to a starting rotation that already included Tim Hudson and Mark Mulder.

Sure enough, Barry delivered. His arrival in Oakland was arguably the final piece of the puzzle, leading to one of the best runs in A's history. For the better part of seven years, Barry delighted A's crowds with the flair, style, grit, and talent he brought to the mound every fifth day. The highlights of his time in an A's uniform are already well documented: six straight seasons of 200-plus innings, 102 wins, a 3.55 ERA, five playoff appearances in seven years, and a Cy Young Award in 2002 at the age of twenty-four when he went 23–5 and dominated the American League from start to finish.

I remember watching Barry strike out the side in his big-league debut. I remember how dominant he was in his Cy Young season of 2002. And I remember everything about his last great start for us in the Metrodome in the 2006 ALDS. Barry, along with Tim and Mark, forever solidified their place in Oakland history as the Big Three.

But there was always more to Barry than just pitching and baseball. He was genuinely interested in the world and in people. In his teammates and in his competitors. His love of music, rooted in his parents' careers, was always evident—he carried a guitar slung over the shoulder of his suits on road trips, and he meticulously curated the clubhouse's pregame setlist on the days he pitched. He was never your typical "ballplayer" and never wanted that tag to define him.

And while that sentiment might not be entirely unique, Barry truly was.

Barry's uniqueness is what brings us back to that story you're about to read. It is a candid and captivating tale of Barry's journey to the big leagues. But it is more than that. Barry takes us back to the beginnings of the Zito family and to the foundation built by his dad, Joe. I was lucky enough to get to know Joe a bit during Barry's years with the A's. He was a devoted husband and father—a man fully invested in his son's baseball career.

In *Curveball*, Barry reveals a complex relationship between father and son, and all the years of work that got him to the major leagues. It is a rare glimpse into what made Barry who he is—a remarkable pitcher and man.

I know you'll enjoy it.

—Billy Beane,
Executive Vice President of Baseball
Operations, Oakland Athletics

Introduction: Fame, Shame, and the Love of the Game

"If San Fran wins the World Series, does Barry Zito get a ring?"

—Fan forum thread on *ProSportsDaily*,
October 20, 2010[1]

Don't you worry, folks! I'm going to single-handedly bring this National League West title home for you!"

I spoke out loud with a huge grin and a mock confidence to all the people I drove past as they were out enjoying the mild fall evening in my beautiful city of San Francisco. After leaving Friday night's series opener in the fourth inning against the San Diego Padres, I was heading home to rest up for my big start the next day.

I had a desperate craving for approval from an entire city that had been angry with me for my poor pitching performance since I joined their home team four years earlier. Could winning the next day erase everyone's memory, including my own? With just one good game, could I trade in my bruised ego and get my team, coaches, fans, and the media back on my side? Maybe even hear some "Zito" chants from our fans again instead of the usual boos and obscenities I had become accustomed to. I wanted to see index fingers pointing number one in my direction instead of middle fingers turned upward at me.

But, honestly, I didn't have the right motives. Not even close. I wasn't going out there to "win it for my boys" or the loyal Giants fans. The only thing that drove me to succeed in my start the next day was the chance to reverse everyone's negative opinions about me.

Approval and Anger

That first weekend in October 2010, neck and neck with the San Diego Padres in the standings, we headed into our final series for a three-game home stand. My scheduled start was the second game on Saturday. If I could lead us to victory, we could clinch the National League West and go to the 2010 playoffs.

I had started that season out strong at 6–1. But then I fell into my familiar nosedive of pitching badly, going 3–11 the rest of the year. Limping to the finish line, I lost eight of my last ten starts. Always looming like a dark cloud overhead were the city's massive expectations. No one felt the weight more than I did.

Leaving the Oakland A's and signing with the Giants in 2007, I'd been given the richest contract ever handed to a pitcher in Major League Baseball. I was making millions of dollars more than any other player on the team. The first three years of the contract had been marred by poor performance, and now here I was again. Pitching my team into the playoffs the next day was my one opportunity for redemption.

Saturday morning, I was at the field by 9:00 a.m., ready to prove I was worth the $18 million I was getting paid that year. But in front of a packed AT&T Park, I failed. Miserably. I walked two batters with the bases loaded in the first inning and from there the downward spiral began. I was pulled out of the game in the fourth inning and we ended up losing 4–2.

Our last hope at making the playoffs was now solely on the shoulders of lefty Johnny Sanchez, the starter for the high-pressure, must-win Sunday matchup. With our 162-game season on the line, Johnny went out and dominated the Padres, getting the win, and leading us to a division championship. We were on our way to the playoffs for the first time in eight years.

Seconds after closer Brian Wilson threw the last pitch of the game past the Padres' Will Venable, the entire team shot out of the dugout. As I charged the field with the guys, questions began swirling in my mind. *What do I have to celebrate? What have I done to help this team? Do I even belong on this field right now?*

With all of us swarming the mound, as soon as the bear hugs and high fives began, I noticed some of my teammates ignoring me, flat out avoiding me as if I were invisible. Paralyzed with rejection, I did my best to act excited while everyone else was going crazy celebrating their big playoff win.

AT&T Park was electrified with thousands of fans waving signs and basking in the sweet payoff of sticking with their team through the ups and downs of September. Something had shifted with the Giants fan base that season and they had transformed from a benign group of baseball enthusiasts into one of the most intimidating home crowds in the game.

Player by player, the team began a victory lap around the entire field, high-fiving fans leaning over the rail. I worked hard to blend into the middle of the pack and made sure I had on my big sunglasses to hide the tears. My team was going to the MLB playoffs, and I was crying out of personal defeat because this victory had nothing to do with me. My pride was on life support. I could not wait to get out of that stadium.

When the on-field celebration with the fans was over and we headed back to the locker room, I felt disoriented as I tried making sense of what was happening to me. In the clubhouse, Visqueen plastic sheeting had been hung wall-to-wall to protect against the imminent explosion of champagne. The attendants had cleared out the tables and sofas to make room for the madness and wheeled in iced-down coolers of bubbly.

When the party began, I took off my sunglasses to purposely make sure my face was covered in champagne to disguise the tears that kept coming. Doing all I could to stay unnoticed, within minutes I heard manager Bruce Bochy's growling, bear-like voice cut through the deafening celebration: "Hey Z! I need you in my office." I turned to see him leaning out into the locker room from the coach's hallway, glaring in my direction.

The cold, hard fact was that by the end of the season, the other four starters on the team were pitching far better than I was. I didn't want to face the decision that my poor performance had forced Bochy to make. Knowing this was the moment of his verdict, I closed my eyes and took a deep breath. *Okay, BZ, here we go.*

I strolled in nonchalantly, as if I didn't know what was coming, catching his eye just long enough to ask, "What's up, Boch?" and then stared back down at the floor.

After letting out a sigh of discomfort, Bochy said in his matter-of-fact tone, "Z, you know this ain't easy for me but we only have room for four starters on the playoff roster, and I've got to go with my top guys right now. You're welcome to stay with us and work out in case someone gets hurt but . . . if you just want to pack up and get out of here, go on home, and get a fresh start next year in spring training, we'll all understand."

His words cut deep. I had no idea I might be left off the playoff roster. And even more shocking was to be told I could just go home while my team pursued their World Series dreams.

But the decision made sense because National League teams have to carry one less pitcher in the playoffs to allow for more position players. I couldn't blame Bochy or the front office. In fact, I couldn't blame *anyone* but myself. No excuses or scapegoats for a Zito, ever.

Repulsed by the thought of retreat, I responded, "But Boch, these are my boys and we live for this. It's why we do what we do. Get to the playoffs and maybe one day to the World Series." I paused to find the right words, but then blurted out, "Go home? Are you kidding?! I'm not going to watch you guys on TV. That's crazy! I'll stay here, stay in shape, and be ready if you need me." I knew my one possible playing scenario was if someone should get hurt and I was needed to fill in at a moment's notice.

Bochy looked a bit surprised by my answer because he knew all the harsh criticism and cruel remarks a multimillion-dollar pitcher cut from the roster would endure from the media and fans throughout the playoffs. But he responded, "Okay. Well, perfect. Get your work in and stay ready, Z. You never know when we'll need you."

I slipped back into the clubhouse, changed into street clothes, and headed out the door. With the chaos of the celebration still going on, I don't think anyone even noticed me leaving. *Dead man walking.*

I knew the players' families, friends, and hangers-on would be packed in the tunnel outside the clubhouse waiting to congratulate everyone. So I went the other direction, back out onto the field and through the gap in the left field fence. From there I snuck into the players' parking lot, avoiding everyone I could. A deep sense of shame enveloped me and I just wanted to escape.

Facing My Father

Later that night, looking for any sign of hope, I texted a Christian teammate who had given me a Bible a couple of years earlier. I typed out: "Hey man, can you give me some helpful verses? Where should I start reading this book?"

He texted back: "From the beginning." *Ouch.*

Feeling like I had no other options, I did the unthinkable. I called my father. With each passing ring my heart raced faster and the lump in my throat grew heavier. When he finally answered, I delivered the news: "Hey Dad. Bochy just told me they're leaving me off the playoff roster."

Admitting to the man who sacrificed everything in his life for me that I had failed miserably was the hardest thing I ever did. But what came next was even more daunting.

"I'm thinking about . . . quitting baseball. But first, I need to know: If I do, would you still love me, Dad?"

The most terrifying thing I could say to my father was that I was *thinking* about quitting baseball because throughout my entire life, playing ball meant I was worthy of Dad's love and approval. Ever since I stepped onto my first mound at six years old, he and I had been a team. As I spoke, memories of our victories throughout the years flashed like a photo album in my mind—from making the varsity in high school, pitching for the University of Southern California, getting drafted as a pro in the first round, and getting called up to the major leagues.

But now with one simple question, I was forcing my father's hand. Was my well-being *really* his greatest concern? Or was there some darker selfish motive driving him to be my personal coach and fiercely dedicated career manager over the last twenty-five years?

Still shell-shocked from Bochy's news, I wasn't even sure I was ready to walk away from the game. But I knew it was time to confront the major strongholds in my life, with my father's influence over me being number one. By questioning the foundation upon which our relationship was built, I was doing all I could to draw a line in the sand to finally separate my will from his. And once and for all earn the freedom to ponder for the first time what life might be like on the other side of baseball for Barry Zito. The truth was I never felt my life was actually mine at all, but in this moment of reckless courage I was doing all I could to take it back.

In his always gentle but straightforward fashion, Dad responded immediately, "Well, Barry, that would not be a wise business decision. But, of course I'd still love you."

The fact that Dad had led his answer with baseball and business instead of his love for me as his son said it all. I can't know for certain what he was actually thinking during such a moment of truth. But what I took from his knee-jerk response was what I had always felt: my baseball career was the most important part of our relationship.

For so long, shame had been a familiar part of me, always by my side. But I couldn't stand its presence in my life any longer and had become desperate to rid myself of the pain.

In Jeremiah 17:9, God said, "The human heart is the most deceitful of all things, and desperately wicked. Who really knows how bad it is?" (NLT). During those waking nightmare days in the fall of 2010, I was beginning to get an unfiltered glimpse of my own heart for the first time—and I did not like what I saw.

Half-Italian, All-American

"If you really want to be great, you have to work for it. It was a matter of pursuing excellence, whatever the situation."

—Joe Zito, *New York Times*[1]

"So, Barry's half-Italian?" the sports reporter asked.

"Yes, and he loves that," my mom answered. "All my kids love the whole idea of being Italian."

Even as a small child, ever since I first heard the stories from my dad about my family heritage, I have always taken great pride in being Italian. But being raised from the age of six totally immersed in "America's national pastime," I've also taken great honor in being all-American.

The Old Country to the New Land

My grandfather, Giuseppe Zito, was born in the late 1800s and raised in Calabria, Italy. He moved up through the ranks in the Italian armed forces and eventually became a four-star general in Benito Mussolini's army. Giuseppe had business experience and

Benito a background in journalism, so the two also became partners and started a newspaper. As my father said when he told me the story, "All this happened before Mussolini went insane."

We have several family photos from that era, one with my grandfather and other generals standing with Mussolini and another of my aunt Rose as a toddler up on her godfather Benito's shoulders. Giuseppe's medals from the Italian army now hang in a frame in my sister's home in Los Angeles.

During a losing battle in the First World War while fighting for Italy, my grandfather was severely wounded and presumed dead. They dragged his body into a lineup of fallen men. As was often done in war to be certain there were no survivors, soldiers of the opposing army systematically walked down the line and bayoneted the dead in the midsection. No need to waste precious bullets just for ensuring their demise.

Miraculously, my grandfather was able to disguise the fact that he was still breathing while being stabbed. After the soldiers left, he crawled away and eventually found help. That event proved my grandfather Giuseppe was indeed a survivor. A character trait I later came to see as hereditary in the Zito family.

The era around both world wars led many Italians to leave their home country because of rampant unemployment and difficult living conditions. Giuseppe and his wife, Katerina (or the American spelling of Katherine), eventually immigrated their family to New York in the mid-1920s. Due to his prewar business experience, Giuseppe was appointed to a high position with the Bank of Italy, which we know today as Bank of America.

The Family Secret

Katherine had children from a previous marriage, so between her own and those she and Giuseppe had, there were a total of seventeen kids. But the seventeenth child, born in 1928, was the couple's last, and arrived in a way no one expected. That year, my grandfather, having an obvious evil streak, raped his fourteen-year-old stepdaughter, Frances. The deed was discovered when she became pregnant. In fear of Giuseppe's shameful act being found out, the family sent Frances away to live with relatives and have the baby.

In September of 1928 immediately following the birth, Frances gave the child up to an orphanage and returned home to live with her mother and stepfather. I can't imagine what it must have been like for her to return to such a precarious living situation.

When the rape of Frances was brought to light, my grandparents remained together, but Katherine insisted they stay in separate rooms and the marriage was understandably never the same. Six months after Frances came back home, Katherine couldn't bear the fact that her first grandchild was living in an orphanage, destined to grow up without blood-related family. She knew in her heart what had happened was no fault of Frances's or the innocent newborn, so she decided to go to the orphanage and bring the baby back home. Katherine raised the child as if it were her own, referring to Frances as the older sister from that point on.

That baby boy was my father, Joseph Zito.

Since everyone in the Bronx community knew that Katherine had not been pregnant, the family hid him from the neighborhood. When anyone came to the house, they placed him in a dresser drawer, and as he got bigger, in a closet in the back room. Dad shared that he had vivid memories that never left him of being hidden away when company was over.

To this day, it is still difficult to imagine what that must have felt like for him.

My father's life was covered in a shroud of shame from day one. Through my own journey of maturity and growth over the years, I came to understand how the spiritual and emotional ties from his life to mine were very real in the need to constantly prove value and self-worth to the outside world.

When Dad was around the age of sixteen, Katherine told him the truth: she was actually his grandmother, and his sister Frances was in fact his mother, just fifteen years older than her son. One of the hardest things for him to understand was that those he believed to be his big sisters and brothers were actually his aunts and uncles. He never suspected anything, so the shock was incredible. As a teenager, my dad had to totally reframe his understanding of family.

I remember when Dad sat me down as a teenager and told me how he came into the world. "Barry, I was born out of wedlock. Although my father had been a war hero, he committed a terrible act with his stepdaughter. Being so young, my mom knew nothing about taking care of a baby, so I was raised by her mother, who was actually my grandmother, and called her Mom the rest of my life." I recall being surprised at how matter-of-fact Dad made the story sound, as if he was talking about another person's life. I imagine he must have had to disconnect from the emotions as a way to move forward past the turbulent environment in which he grew up.

AKA Drake Holloway

After the eighth grade, Dad made the difficult decision to not return to school but go to work to help his family. Around the same time, he started playing piano as a hobby but soon began to see music as his ticket out of poverty. By his late teens, he was playing professionally around New York City. But knowing in that day his Italian heritage could be a roadblock to an entertainment career, he took on the stage name of Drake Holloway. In his own words, the name was "as White-Anglo-Saxon-Protestant as I could possibly think of."

Dad's growing reputation as a composer and musical director got the attention of artists such as Duke Ellington and Frank Sinatra. He also arranged music for the Ed Sullivan and Red Skelton TV shows. At one point, he took in musician Charlie "Bird" Parker when he was down and out—before the sax player's big break. Dad even once rehearsed Marilyn Monroe for a song she sang in one of her films. He was obviously playing in his own version of the big leagues.

My father's breakthrough moment in the music industry came when both Frank Sinatra and Nat King Cole wanted to hire him as the arranger and composer for their big bands. Carefully considering the reputation of each man, Dad chose to go with Nat. In my father's own words, "Nat was a man of high character." Dad's job of arranging and conducting full-time for Cole's band allowed for his family to do very well.

Lyrics Meet Melody

In the early 1960s, an attractive nineteen-year-old singer belted out the classic song "Summertime" at a Hollywood audition and booked her first national gig. Soon after, she arrived in New York to rehearse with a vocal group for an upcoming tour. When the seasoned musical director walked in to start practice, he quickly noticed the young lady standing with her back to him. Even before seeing her face, he knew this woman was something special. Once she turned around and looked into his eyes, he was immediately lovestruck.

Mom said the moment Dad walked into that rehearsal room wearing his baby-blue suit, she was instantly captivated by the way he commanded the room. *Yep, that was Joe Zito.*

That's how my parents met. My mother began singing backup for Nat King Cole, while my father was his bandleader.

My mother, Roberta, was raised in a strong Christian family in

San Diego who were all very musically talented. Her mother was also a professional singer. After high school, Mom went to UCLA for a year and then dropped out to sing in Nat's traveling music group known as the Merry Young Souls.

Even though Dad was fifteen years older, they pursued a relationship, fell in love, and got married. Evidently the day Dad went to her hometown to ask for her hand in marriage, he encountered some obvious resistance. Although my mother was clearly in love, her father, Bill, could not see past the fact that his daughter's boyfriend was a New York Italian, and much older. However, in typical Joe Zito fashion, he eventually earned Bill's blessing and married Roberta soon after.

After two years of singing with Nat, Mom left the band because she was pregnant. In spite of Dad's success, my father always wanted more. He didn't enjoy being "Nat's guy," as he put it, but wanted to be "his own man," composing classical music like his heroes, Rachmaninoff and Mozart. So my mother was totally shocked when my father decided to give up the security of leading Nat's band to begin composing classical concertos. Since he had never saved up any money, hard times came quickly.

So with my oldest sister, Bonnie, about to be born, they now had no income. Throughout their entire lives, finances were a constant battle. Because of his metaphysical belief in "attracting success by appearing successful," Dad often had the best tailors in New York City create custom leisure suits in all his favorite colors. My sisters recalled to me that Mom often lost her temper with Dad because financially, he was "living in a fantasy world." So when he made good money, he spent too much, and when he wasn't making any, he still spent too much.

In 1965, along with their newborn daughter, they had to move into his mother's New York apartment. After four long years of no real success in the classical world, Dad realized he had to provide for his family and began to educate himself in the field of entertainment law. He bought volumes of books on the subject and studied them into the wee hours of the morning.

My dad devised a new plan and was preparing for his next act.

What Happens in Vegas

Four years after Bonnie, my sister Sally was born, with our family still poor and struggling. A few months later, Dad decided to leave New York and move the family cross-country to Las Vegas to become a talent manager. With his entertainment connections, street smarts, and newly acquired legal skills, he began to do very well in "the live entertainment capital of the world." But he also started living even further above his means for appearance's sake.

While Dad took out a line of credit to retile the entire kitchen, my mother and sisters had to spend hours looking through the house for nickels and dimes to buy food. Just to eat their next meal, the three of them searched everywhere, from the couch cushions to the car, for spare change.

But my father finally found success once again in his new career in a new city. Before long, my family had a huge home in the very prestigious Scotch Eighties neighborhood. Hotel mogul Steve Wynn and legendary comedian Buddy Hackett were neighbors and friends. On the surface, they were doing great and Dad was killing it in talent management.

Then on May 13, 1978, I, Barry William Zito, came into the world when Bonnie was thirteen and Sally was nine.

Although he was quite the hustler, there was a tender side to my father that he didn't allow many people to see. I have vivid memories of Dad walking me around our front yard on warm evenings, swaying me back and forth in his arms, singing a special song he had written for me: "Barry William is a nice boy, yes he is." After singing to me, he pointed up at the sky and said, "The moon, the moon," as I repeated the words after him. I felt so safe in his arms. The sweet melody of that song was branded on my heart, and to this day, I sing it each night to my children with their names in place of mine.

One other vivid memory is of my family driving my father to the airport for another one of his business trips. Dad was always dressed in a fancy three-piece suit with freshly shined black leather shoes and a perfectly tied tie.

The appearance of success and wealth was extremely important to Dad while our family and home were far from the picture-perfect life he projected. For example, after my family sold their big Vegas house for $292,000 after buying the property five years earlier for $80,000, he had to use all the equity to pay off existing debt. But then Dad still decided to spend thousands of dollars remodeling their next house, a rental, so the front of the home looked impeccable, even though the inside was barely livable. That decision was a metaphor for our lives.

While living in Vegas, Mom found out that Dad had lied about his age and he was actually three years older than what he told her when they first met. She also found out he wasn't actually raised on a farm in upstate New York. He was so ashamed of where he actually grew up on 168th Street in the Bronx that he didn't want her to know.

After thirteen years in Nevada, my family was drawn toward the West Coast. For one, with both my sisters now teenagers, a change of scenery offered an opportunity to escape the drug culture spreading across Vegas during the 1980s. And another situation unfolding was that my father was in debt to "certain people in town," and they were losing their patience with his excuses.

Dad sold everything we owned to pay back outstanding debts, like his coveted black Lincoln Continental for $6,000 in cash and even our two family dogs. *When a man sells his favorite ride and his dog, you know something is up.*

The last factor was that the New Age church my grandmother founded in San Diego was flourishing, and she needed my mom's help to run the International Center there. But this requires some backstory on Mom's family.

A Dramatic Deception

My maternal grandmother, Ann, came from a very normal Christian home. She was extremely intelligent and became an accomplished singer, pianist, and composer, focusing her talents on the opera in New York. She married and had my mom and three other children.

In 1954, they moved to San Diego, where Ann stayed involved in opera and the local arts community. Singing regularly at the San Diego Church of Religious Science and always having a fascination with spirituality, she began to study the theology and beliefs of that church and became a licensed religious science practitioner in 1960.

Ann bought in fully to these beliefs that were vastly different from her Christian upbringing—that Jesus was not God's Son and that every person could be a "Christ" if they could only remove the obstacles in themselves that prevented their true godly nature from surfacing. Unlike her Christian roots, this newfound teaching claimed that people could more or less save themselves if they implemented enough self-control.

What happened next will sound peculiar to most of you, and even though I have heard this story throughout my life, it still sounds strange to me.

In her book *Who Is with Me*, my grandmother Ann wrote about two events taking place in 1962 that changed the course of her life. One Saturday riding the city bus, she felt that a person nearby was somehow mentally communicating with her. She turned and saw a slim, older man sitting in what appeared to be a pool of white light. Although she attempted to dismiss the mysterious intrusion, Ann felt he was somehow eavesdropping on her thoughts. She never spoke to him and, after getting off the bus, walked home like any other day.

Six months later on the evening of October 19, 1962, my grandmother and my grandfather Bill attended a classical concert. A handsome, older gentleman came and took the seat next to her. Ann began to feel strong sensations of love and warmth, soon realizing they were somehow exuding from this stranger next to her. She felt as if he nonverbally communicated to her mind but she was now able to communicate back in the same manner.

Ann goes on to explain in her book how she had an incredible exchange of power and love with this man solely in the mental realm, while she sat in silence watching the show with her husband. When the opera ended, my grandparents went home with no words ever spoken to the mystery man.

The next morning my grandmother was a changed woman. The strange man was still communicating to her from within her mind, and she also realized he was the same person from the bus. But this time, he had returned with a spiritual message for her.

Seeking guidance during a channeling session with a parapsychology teacher, Ann began communicating internally with the spirit of an ancient Hindu master who said her purpose was to start this new teaching, but that first "there is going to be great change in your life." Ann somehow knew he meant she must divorce her husband. Though physically and emotionally in love, their marriage had been growing apart spiritually over the years. When she told Bill she had to leave him, sadly, my grandpa's response was, "I always knew I was going to lose you."

My grandmother claims she fully submitted to this "higher message," divorced her husband, and committed her life to the declaration of this teaching to the world. My grandfather Bill held a grudge against his ex-wife until the day he died, because he could never fully understand the life choices she had made.

Ann eventually called this message "Teaching of the Inner Christ," using the acronym T.I.C. The bottom line of the belief system is that everyone is a "unique individual Christ after the example of Jesus." In 1963, she met and married the man that had been promised to her. She and her new mate, Pete Meyer, formed "The Society for the Teaching of the Inner Christ."

When I was only five years old, my mom took me to my first "Inner Christ counseling" where my counselor gave me the name of my "Inner Christ." Early in my childhood, I recall seeing a silhouette in the hallway outside my room of a small being, and I interpreted that to be him. My mom said I could call on him anytime I was sad or afraid.

These are the spiritual beliefs I grew up with as a child. I have no idea if my grandmother's experiences were real or if she suffered some kind of delusion. But one thing I do know, she dedicated her entire life to these teachings and believed them with her whole heart. Because of her unique purpose and, as I was told, "divine disposition," I never called her any typical grandparent name. I just called her Ann all my life. To say she was vastly different from the typical grandmother is an understatement.

California Dreamin'

With a fresh start for the family on the horizon, we packed up our home in Las Vegas into two large tractor trailers and headed west to El Cajon, California. Mom became the new pastor and cofounder of T.I.C., and once we got settled, she became fully immersed in the church, often working there seven days a week.

The move was a major paradigm shift for our family. Dad was having a hard time figuring out how to monetize his skills in entertainment while living in a "dead town" as he called it. With Sally now fifteen years old and Bonnie nineteen, they were nearing their independence. Mom was gone all the time and Dad was always at home.

But in this change of season, he had a brand-new prospect on which to focus: Barry in baseball.

Let the Games Begin

"We've got video from back then. This little kid, long hair, enormous glove, throwing that curveball, guys swinging and missing."

—Roberta Zito, *SF Gate*[1]

Bam! Nailed it!" Find another rock and do it again. Cock my left arm back, lock in the target, and throw. "Yes! Got it." Another rock, another direct hit. And another. And another. Down the line I go. "This is soooooo fun. I could do this all day."

Like any five-year-old boy does when bored and wandering around in his backyard by himself, I invented a new game with what I had available. I noticed how Mom had incrementally lined the empty clothespins along the fifteen-foot cables stretched between two posts. Finding a handful of just-the-right-size-for-my-hand rocks, I began to pick off her pins on the line one by one. Sure, I missed a couple, but I not only hit most of them on the first try, I also hit them hard enough to knock them clean off into the grass. I didn't realize in the moment that I was "good at it," because I was just having fun watching them fly off like tiny missiles being launched into space.

What I did not know was that Dad had walked by a back window just as I had come out of my windup releasing another rock. Seeing the clothespin fly off the line, he stopped to watch. After several more successful throws, sporting a big, proud-father grin, he called Mom to join him. I had tried football and soccer when we lived in Vegas but never loved either of them. They stood in the window watching me perfect my new game. After Dad saw my consistent accuracy with the rocks and clothespins, he offered the obvious to my mother: "Roberta, why don't we let Barry try baseball?"

When I was six years old, I got my first ball and glove. That's when everything changed. Dad felt a strong connection to something he saw in me. A new element was added to our relationship once he observed me working passionately, just like he had done for so many years with his music.

Our parallel lines transformed into a triangle—father, son, and baseball.

The talent manager in him smelled raw potential. Dad already had the skill set to disciple and develop artists but now he was able to utilize that in a new way by helping his son in an activity completely outside of music. But my father was always as much a student as a teacher, so studying a totally new paradigm became a fresh challenge for him.

Since I loved throwing the baseball in our backyard so much, my parents signed me up for a T-ball league in La Mesa. I vividly remember that first day on the field. Having never set foot on a baseball diamond before, I quickly ran out to the middle of that white chalk circle surrounding the pitcher's mound as if something was calling me out there.

A typical day for me in grade school was to come home after class, eat a quick snack as Dad finished up the day's work, and then go out to the backyard with him and spend the next two hours practicing. We were out there *every* single day of the year, even weekends, except for sick days and holidays. The weather in Southern California is some of the best in the country to accommodate a year-round sports commitment.

Dedication to my daily practice sessions was easy for my dad because he was obsessively routine-oriented. To illustrate, one example I recall is every morning he ate his favorite brand of banana nut muffins along with his Pero coffee replacement. The only store that sold those muffins was Price Club (now Costco). But he found out they were going to discontinue his go-to breakfast food.

So Dad went to the store, found the manager, and using his amazing charm convinced the guy to give him the owner's personal phone number. He then returned home, got the owner on the line, and told him why he needed to continue carrying that particular type of muffin. Whatever Dad said worked because he was able to keep his *exact* breakfast routine for years. He also ended up being friends with the owner from that day on.

If he needed to get something done, Dad never messed with anyone down the line. He always went straight to the source, even the CEO at times. From muffins to major league contracts, it didn't matter: Joe Zito did whatever it took to get what he wanted.

Me Becomes We

Dad spared no expense or energy to get the best of whatever I needed to improve at baseball. If a new book or instruction manual was released, he bought a copy immediately. When Tom Seaver's *The Art of Pitching* came out, there were detailed pictures in sequence of how to throw specific pitches. When I was seven, I started studying the diagrams for how to throw a curveball. As is typical, the pictures showed right-handed versions. But being left-handed, I had to grip the ball opposite of the photo, the reverse of what was shown.

I must have incorrectly transcribed the book photos from right-handed to left-handed, because I gripped my curveball in a unique way that no one had ever seen before. Every other pitcher I knew clamped down on the seam of the baseball with their middle finger but I used my index finger instead. I am not sure why my curve dropped as much as it did but I am convinced I had better control of the pitch because of the way I gripped the ball.

For those first few years there wasn't much room to play catch in our small, sloping backyard, so I used a pitch-back net to throw into. But when I was eight years old, we moved from El Cajon to a home in nearby La Mesa. Our new backyard was flat and rectangular at around sixty-five feet long. Dad buried a two-by-four halfway into the ground so only the top was above the dirt. It was exactly forty-six feet away from a plastic plate that sat in front of an old mattress we leaned against the back fence.

Even at sixty years old, Dad had the energy to work with me in the backyard for hours each day. To begin our practice sessions, he took me through advanced stretching routines. We played light catch for a while, and then once I was ready to take the mound, he'd strap on the bright red catcher's gear that he couldn't afford but purchased anyway. Looking like a real catcher, he sat right behind the rubber home plate on a plastic white bucket flipped upside down.

Sometimes Dad played classical records like Rachmaninoff's Piano Concerto no. 2 through the living room speakers, opening all the back windows so we could hear the music. With the video camera running, I did my practice routine of throwing sixty to one hundred pitches, depending on what we needed to work on that day. Some days when Dad felt too fatigued, I threw to a strike zone painted on an old queen-sized mattress.

Most kids at my age only threw a fastball and changeup, so throwing a left-handed curveball set me apart early. Hitters I faced could rarely make solid contact against a fastball so my big, looping pitch often confused them, made evident by their awkward swings. At eleven years old, I made my first all-star team. I wasn't a starter but got to back up in a big game when the pitcher was hit with a line drive and came out. I pitched five innings in relief, and we won. That drew attention to me in our league and provided my first taste of standing out from my peers.

When Dad had been a talent manager, he had always been very protective of his clients and started applying that principle to me. For example, on game days when I was pitching, he instructed Mom and my sisters not to talk to me. He wanted to shield me from any distractions to fully focus on the upcoming game. Before we left the house for the field, he warmed me up in the backyard, having me throw several dozen pitches to be certain I was ready.

Back then, I just assumed that my dad somehow already knew everything about pitching, but years later he confessed that he often stayed up at night to learn the new material he planned to teach me the next day. He was literally just one step ahead of me all the time. That explained why I often saw his handwritten notes in the margins of the pitching books to remind him of what to show me.

Dad videotaped every game with a VHS camera. Back at home we watched to critique my delivery by taking elaborate notes on which pitching mechanics needed to be improved. When the four-head VCR came out, my sister Bonnie got us one for Christmas, likely from Dad's suggestion. By playing back game tapes on a four-head machine, for the first time ever I could watch my delivery frame by frame. That was a major turning point in my development as a pitcher.

With Dad and me both committed 110 percent to my baseball career, there was a subtle point where he began to refer to *me* as *we*. He became too attached, even to the point of saying things like, "When *we* are on the mound . . ." But anytime Mom heard him use those phrases, she quickly corrected him by saying, "Joe! It's not you on the mound; it's Barry." But the "we" carried all the way into my major league career. Through books, curriculum, weekend camps, constant drills, and private lessons, we were "leaving no stone unturned," as Dad always said, doing everything we could for me to improve at baseball.

As a result of the tunnel vision at such a young age, two things happened inside me. One, I was further and further insulated from the outside world, and two, life was more and more about baseball. My identity as a person was becoming fused to my identity as a ballplayer.

Dad unknowingly cemented into my impressionable mind that I was only worthy of his love and acceptance when I performed well on the mound. After good games, I received praise and nods of approval. "See, Barry, you *are* a great champion." But after tough games, he looked frustrated and in a low, almost whispering tone said, "Barry, we've got work to do." At that point, my sense of self-worth became directly connected to my pitching performance, which, of course, changed from game to game. The amount of love I received literally depended on what I *did*, not *who* I was.

All that said, I don't believe Dad ever had any ill intentions. He wasn't purposefully trying to create a performance-based relationship. But along the way, he lost sight of where he ended and I began, and so did I. In a very real way, *my* career became *his* career.

Expanding Team Zito

When I was twelve, Dad found a personal pitching coach. Randy Jones had won the coveted Cy Young Award playing for the Padres in the mid-70s. Randy was offering private lessons in his backyard in Poway for fifty dollars a session. Dad and Mom drove the mountain back roads to Randy's house each week for my hour of training. Dad set up the tripod and camera to record the entire lesson. Back at home, we watched the tape and took notes to reinforce that day's instruction.

I went to Randy's house every week for four straight years. The money, time, and energy invested in me were beginning to add up. Throughout this entire season of my childhood, Dad was trying to create music in his small home studio, while Mom was at the church every day. But with Dad unable to make much money, Mom was the sole breadwinner. We had $1,050 a month on which to live from her minister's allowance. They clearly could not afford the $200 per month plus gas money for those lessons, but somehow they always managed to make them work. On the other side of all the sacrifice was the fact that my pitching was constantly improving.

As I progressed from Little League to Pony (middle school age) into high school, I was not the standout I hoped to be. I never threw very hard and could rarely overpower anyone. Those skills came later. Coming from a family of musicians, I was really not that athletic by nature and was always a bit chubby. I didn't lose the extra weight until later in high school when I started to get my height.

I eventually worked my way up from the freshman team to JV (junior varsity). Although I wanted to play varsity as a sophomore, I wasn't good enough and had to wait until my junior year. I could never hit too well, either, so that ended when I was on the freshman team.

Even though I wasn't the best player at my school, I was just good enough to join travel ball teams over the summers. I wasn't the star but played more of a supporting role as my club teams advanced to the Connie Mack, Colt, and Palomino World Series on a national stage three years in a row. Although my personal performance was helpful at best, my parents always told me that I was the "special ingredient" that propelled the team's success.

Becoming a Baller

With my total focus on baseball, I didn't have the typical social life that my teenage peers enjoyed. Living in sunny Southern California with the beach just a short drive away, I was often too consumed with pitching to take advantage of our location. The few friends I did manage to make were most often the tough crowd, the wrong crowd. Wanting so badly to be cool and have an identity off the field, I hung out with the troublemakers. To escape the daily grind of baseball, I wanted to be around only nonathletes when given the choice.

I think because of my religious practice schedule, when I did get the time to hang out, I wanted to release all that pent-up energy and angst that normal teens have. I didn't want what little social life I had to be on the straight and narrow path. I craved freedom outside of my highly disciplined baseball life and rebelled against structure anytime I could.

With the constant pressure from sports, I eventually started smoking pot. Seeing I could make some money, I began to sell as well. But before long I realized there were better profits in harder drugs, so I quickly moved into that world.

Even though I was totally committed to baseball, I was not at all the American apple pie kid many people may have thought I was from watching me on the field. Like my father in his early years, I was learning the art of appearance. I was hanging out with stoners, skaters, and gang members. I spent most of my free time either on drugs or in the rough parts of town, or both.

As a student, keeping all my energy on baseball and partying, I managed to somehow maintain a C average. My high school baseball coach knew I was involved with the street kids, so he took every opportunity he could to let me know he didn't like me. He reprimanded me in front of the team any time he could to "teach me a lesson."

The worst of his episodes was when I was pitching on a road

game against Santana High School. With a runner on second base, I gave up a base hit to right field but forgot to run behind home plate to back up the throw from the outfield. The fielder's throw got past the catcher, exposing my mistake. Before the play had ended, the coach was already sprinting right at me, yelling every cussword in the book. Every last shred of my pride withered as his tirade became a spectacle. Then he dismissed me from the field without a word by pointing to the dugout and staring at me until I got the message and walked off.

My first car was a 1976 Monte Carlo that my brother-in-law bought for me for five hundred dollars. The car had chrome rims and twelve-inch subwoofers in the back seat that blended in perfectly with the neighborhoods where I was cruising. I was constantly lying to my parents about what I was doing, where I was, and whom I was with.

One night when I was sixteen, two friends and I were driving back from the beach on the interstate passing by downtown San Diego. I had some weed and a pipe sitting out in the front seat. We began to hear the rattling of loose lug nuts on the right front wheel and quickly pulled off into a rough area of town looking for a gas station.

Driving downtown for the first time, I saw a big, blacked-out van heading straight toward us. Realizing I was going the wrong way on a one-way street, I whipped a right turn into the next alley and continued our search for a gas station, pulling in to one a few blocks later. As soon as I got out of the car, a policeman placed me in a firm headlock. I felt a gun pushing against my temple. They yelled, "Police! On the ground now!" Within moments, they handcuffed us and laid us facedown on the concrete.

The officers picked us up and threw us into their black van, the same one I had avoided on the street minutes earlier, which turned out to be an undercover police vehicle. They quickly found the weed and pipe in the front seat, but also several other bags I had stashed in the trunk, a clear indication to them I was dealing. And this was, of course, long before "medicinal and recreational" marijuana was legal in California.

After they carted us down to the police station and threw us into jail, Mom came to the station to get me at about four in the morning. More heartbroken than upset, she too often gave me the benefit of the doubt because she loved me so much. I constantly took advantage of her trust by telling lies to get out of trouble. On the drive home I made up a crazy story of how I had picked up a hitchhiker earlier that day who had put some things in my trunk before he got in my car. Then when I let him out, he left the drugs in there. Mom believed that I was the innocent victim of a forgetful, druggie hitchhiker, bless her soul.

As a consequence of my arrest, my parents took me in for a weekly drug test at the local hospital that cost them eighty dollars each time. Just more money they did not have. The first week when testing time rolled around, I was high so I grabbed some yellow food coloring from our kitchen and put it into my pocket. At the lab in the bathroom, I ran warm tap water and mixed some of that food coloring into the tube, shook it up, and handed it over. Somehow, and I assume tests are much more accurate these days, my "sample" showed to be negative every week for a year. "Nope, no THC detected in this liquid. He's good."

I had smoked pot for the first time when I was fourteen. As I got older, more independent, and more rebellious, I progressed, or maybe digressed is a better word, to LSD, mushrooms, cocaine, and even crystal meth. In the Southern California drug culture, I pretty much tried everything I could get my hands on.

To my parents' credit, they made every effort to keep me off drugs and on the right path. Although I never came clean because I felt remorse, I had to let them into my hidden life at one point so they could help save my baseball reputation. The summer after my junior year, I made the US Olympic Festival team. There were random drug tests, and I assumed they had better testing than the local hospital. Knowing if I tested positive my baseball future might be ruined, I confessed to my parents that I had crystal meth in my system. Dad sought out the best homeopathic cleanse he could find for me to take. But after each of the four games I played that summer, the drug testers never called my name.

Another close call was when a big group of my friends went to an abandoned neighborhood that was going to be demolished so a freeway could be built. We took backpacks filled with fireworks up to those vacant houses, started breaking out windows, and shot off bottle rockets inside them. About twenty minutes later, we saw a police car creeping up toward the house. We dropped everything and scattered like cockroaches, running as fast and far as we could.

Just as we thought we had escaped, we jumped a fence and there was a cop right in front of us with his gun drawn. After walking us back to my Monte Carlo, he searched through the car. What he did *not* find were the ten little meth rocks wrapped in foil that I had hidden inside a cassette tape case. Had the officer found that stash, my life might have turned out very differently. Instead, he just found a bag of bottle rockets and firecrackers and let us off with a warning.

I began stealing and vandalizing to prove that I could fit in with the misfits. I felt like I was part of something bigger when the kids that were too cool for everyone else accepted me. All that behavior was just my way of having something that *I alone* could control. I felt empowered having a secret place that Dad had no say over, since baseball ran most of my life.

All the while, an overarching belief I had been taught in the spiritual center that my grandmother founded and where my mother pastored was that I was ultimately the one responsible for my own success and happiness. No matter the circumstances, only one person determined my victories and failures—Barry. I wasn't aware at the time but a life-is-all-about-me mind-set began to drive my developing ego.

With my parents' growing concern for the crowd I was hanging out with and also knowing my high school baseball coach had it out for me, the summer before my senior year they decided the time had come for a change of scenery. Dad began looking into private schools in the area that had good baseball programs.

The Right Time to Hit Reset

Dad visited the University of San Diego High School (known as Uni to the locals), which was a Catholic school where all students attended Mass every Friday. Telling the "right people" about my pitching skills, they somehow secured funding for me to join their team. So I transferred to Uni my senior year of high school. Dad figured out a way to separate me from my drug issues while finding a competitive team with a coach that had no preconceived notions about me.

At the Catholic school, my circle of friends became drastically different. I had sworn off all drugs except the occasional toke. As is true with so many people, marijuana was my gateway drug that started me down that path of rampant experimentation and became the last thing to go three long years later. Through that final year of high school, I completely cleaned up my act and prepared for the next steps in my career.

Just in time.

I made a clean break in every way my senior year. No drugs. No dealing. No partying. No bad friends. I had a full-on focus toward academics and baseball. In private school, there were no cliques or color barriers like in public school. There was an unspoken code of respect between all the kids. For the very first time in my life, people liked me. I had friends that really cared, and even better, girls actually talked to me. That was my first experience of being accepted, not because of baseball or rebellious behavior, but just for who I was. I had a great year on all fronts.

Our Uni baseball team won the conference championship in 1996, and I had a solid season. The big curveball was still my signature pitch and some pro scouts were even taking notice, the beginning of a new era in the "we" of my baseball career.

Over the years as any normal boy growing up, I protested to my dad about the strict practice regimen. I wanted to do the typical guy things like go camping on the beach or have a sleepover with friends. While I rarely took part in outside activities, Dad rode the line really well between taskmaster and father, being sure he didn't squeeze all the love out of the sport for me. While I most certainly rebelled, I never rebelled against baseball.

You Still Want This?

Periodically after I gave him some resistance, Dad sat me down for a re-up conversation, asking, "Barry, do you still want to do this?"

I always answered, "Dad, I want to play in the majors one day, so yes, I'm in."

He typically responded, "Okay, if you want to be a major league champion, it's going to take sacrifice and hard work."

"Yeah, I know, Dad. I'm in."

The conversation usually concluded with, "Okay, Barry, I'm going to hold you to that."

And he always did.

As each of my adolescent years passed, baseball became less of a game and more of a profession. By my senior year in high school, baseball being a "kids' game" came to a close. I was getting ready to enter a world where every decision was critical and every move mattered to create a career where I could toe the mound at the highest level for the world to see.

At least that was *our* plan.

Barry's Basics—First Base

Whether you're a superfan or know very little about the game of baseball, I want to give you my personal take on some common terms and give you a bit of inside information. As we move through my story, I will use four total "Barry's Basics" sections—from first base to home plate—to interject other important baseball information for you in my own words.

Let's get started with some information on pitchers and pitching.

Wins, Losses, and ERA

In baseball, whenever you see a pitcher's name mentioned, you'll typically also see his win-loss record. But many people don't know that this is not an accurate indication of how well that pitcher is performing. For a pitcher to get a win, he needs his team's offense to score more runs than he is allowing the other team to score. This is almost completely out of his control. One pitcher could give up eight runs for the win while another could give up one run and get a loss.

A statistic that better indicates a pitcher's performance is ERA, which stands for Earned Run Average. Since a baseball game is nine innings, an average is formulated for how many earned runs a pitcher is allowing over a nine inning span. Earned runs, unlike unearned runs, are not a result of a fielding error by the defense, but are "legitimately" given up by the pitcher. For example, if he throws six innings and allows three earned runs, that's like averaging 4.5 earned runs allowed over nine innings, giving him an ERA of 4.50.

To determine a pitcher's earned run average over the course of a season, you multiply the total earned runs allowed by nine and divide that number by total innings pitched. So if he throws 185 innings in a season and his earned runs on the season are 67, then you multiply 67 times 9, which is 603, then divide that by 185 (total innings pitched) for a 3.26 ERA. Dominant pitchers will usually have an ERA in the twos and low threes, while struggling pitchers will have an ERA in the high fours and fives.

Pitches

I'll start with the pitch I'm most known for. In throwing a curveball, rotation is everything. The faster the ball rotates, the more it breaks downward. The pitch has the *appearance* of moving straight down, which is where the term "12 to 6 curveball" originated. But the ball will always have some horizontal movement also.

Any pitch that doesn't travel straight is called a breaking ball, but the curveball isn't the only type. A slider is similar to a curve but is thrown harder and has even more side-to-side movement. For the hitter, a slider will appear to be a fastball for a longer period of time than a curveball. Having a smaller break, a slider has a higher chance of being thrown for a strike and therefore is a safer pitch to throw in general.

A lot of coaches don't like teaching kids to throw a curveball because the pitch has a lower probability of being called a strike. The strike zone is an invisible three-dimensional box that loosely spans the seventeen-inch width of home plate from the batter's knees to his belly button, depending on the umpire's discretion, of course. A curveball starts high above the strike zone and enters down into the zone from a much steeper angle than a slider. That is exactly why a curveball can fool an umpire into thinking the ball never actually entered the strike zone.

A cutter, or cut fastball, is like a slider but with even less break, which is why it's a better strike percentage pitch than either a curveball or slider.

Sandy Koufax made the curveball famous in the 1960s. When I was coming up in the game, throwing a curveball seemed to be a dying art. So by throwing one left-handed, I was in a very small minority of pitchers. Today, because of the difficulty for hitters to make solid contact with the ball, the curveball is making somewhat of a comeback.

Signals

A lot of people ask me about signals to and from the pitcher. In high school and college, coaches are basically calling every pitch. The catcher gets the signal from the coach and then signals to the pitcher. In the rare circumstances when the coach doesn't call the pitches, the catcher gets a feel for the pitcher's arsenal and calls what he sees fit. But in that scenario, the pitcher still has the final say on what he will throw. He can accept it or shake his head no until the catcher calls the pitch he desires. The importance of the agreement between the pitcher and catcher is so that, for his own safety, the catcher can prepare himself to catch the specific pitch being thrown.

In the pros, coaches no longer call pitches. Big league catchers have a good feel for working hitters and are right there at the plate to pick up on any little clues that can help the pitcher's cause. So if the catcher sees a batter scoot up in the box anticipating an off-speed pitch, he can call a fastball. Being sixty feet away, a pitcher can't see those little details, so the catcher's baseball IQ is important to observe and adjust accordingly. You usually trust a veteran catcher, but call your own game with a young guy.

An important aspect to keep in mind with *all* pro sports is you essentially have a group of independent contractors playing together. So in baseball, one of the ways this plays out is the pitcher ultimately makes his own calls on what he will throw. Each player is essentially in charge of his own career.

3

The Point of Release Is Everything

"We were out in the backyard seven days a week from when he was eight until he went to college. Because I didn't know any other way."

—Joe Zito, *SF Gate*[1]

In the fall of 1995, during my senior year in high school, Dad hired Jeff Riolo, who specialized in presenting players to prospective universities with the goal of landing a baseball scholarship. Finding the right school is an integral part of the path to the major leagues. Jeff put together my first press kit with a headshot, stats, bio, and everything a school required to consider a potential player.

Because of how difficult finances were for my parents, a full-ride scholarship was my only hope of a university education. But for any chance of a future in pro ball, I needed a roster spot at a school with a competitive baseball program. Players do get drafted and signed straight out of high school, but the road to the majors in that scenario is much longer and the chances of survival are minimal.

When Jeff was done, three schools had made offers: the University of California at Santa Barbara, California State University Northridge in Los Angeles, and Wake Forest University in Winston-Salem, North

Carolina. My decision of where to go came down to the fact that I didn't want to live across the country. Santa Barbara was a beautiful campus right on the beach and only a four-hour drive from home. Perfect. So I signed my letter of intent with UC Santa Barbara.

Smooth Talkers with Stopwatches

The major league baseball scouting system is the path by which talent gets discovered all over the world. Each scout works in his defined geographic area and tries to sign the next World Series star for his organization. If his team should win the Series, he receives a big, sparkly ring of his own. In Southern California, an area scout's territory spanned from the Mexican border all the way north to Orange County. The next tier up was a West Coast scout and then a national cross-checker.

The majority of these guys were classic characters like something right out of a movie, old school in both their attitudes and straw hats with a radar gun and stopwatch always within reach. During my senior year, scouts that fit that description started coming to our house to talk to us. A typical conversation was, "At 82 mph, Barry's velocity isn't there yet. But we like his height and love his curveball. We think he can blossom into a solid player." At that point, I was just north of six foot, eventually landing at around six foot four.

Scouts want to know one thing in those meetings: how "sign-able" you are. They need to assess whether your commitment is ultimately to a baseball career or a college education. After all, these guys work for pro teams, not universities. Basically, the thought process is: if our organization is going to burn one of our precious draft picks on you, then we need to know if you are open to playing for us *now*, as opposed to waiting a few years until you are finally draft-eligible again after your junior year in college.

But Dad responded to every scout with the same message: "Well, we see Barry being a top-five-round pick right now, and if he isn't and he goes to college, we feel he will be a first-round pick." At that point the scout got a bit snarky and came back with a disagreeing, yet polite, counter, "Mr. Zito, that's just not going to happen." Back then the guys that went in the top five rounds were throwing a minimum of 90 mph.

Dad, always direct and outspoken, made it clear I was going to school for at least the next three years and continuing to develop into a top-tiered college player. The parting shot from the scouts was a remark such as, "Yes sir, that's what every parent and player feels will happen at this point. Thanks for your time."

But one scout was different from the others. Craig Weissmann from the Seattle Mariners came to visit. When I first met him, he reminded me of Sam Malone, the cocky, witty bartender Ted Danson so artfully portrayed on the TV show *Cheers*. In May, just before my high school graduation, Craig sat down in our living room, looked Dad in the eye, and said, "Look, we want Barry in the eighth round. We can give him a signing bonus of $50,000." He then looked over at me and asked, "So Barry, will you sign with the Mariners?"

Unlike my sisters, I only had memories of being poor. At that point I could not imagine $50,000 even being used in the same sentence as Barry Zito. I got a surge of adrenaline, swallowed hard, and then looked at Dad, knowing better than to say anything or show any response. But being the hard-core talent negotiator, my dad never deviated from his plan or hesitated in the least. He answered for me, "Craig, I'm sorry. We won't be signing for 50,000 bucks."

My father knew that by being a high draft pick and receiving big money up front, the team had more of an interest in that player getting to the major leagues. If the player struggled along the way, the team was less likely to cut him because of losing their financial investment. But if a player was a late-round draft pick and only got a plane ticket to go play, the team had nothing to lose by cutting ties if he should have a tough season.

Continuing his speech to Craig, Dad said, "We've decided Barry is going to Santa Barbara. We believe he can be the top draft pick in the country three years from now." Craig worked hard not to roll his eyes, politely thanked us for our time, and left.

But then a peculiar thing happened.

A few days later, Craig called back and said, "Hey, Mr. Zito, listen, I love Barry. I think he's a good kid. But I see some mechanical flaws in his delivery that I think I can help him with. As you well know, as an employee of the Seattle Mariners, I'm not allowed to work with any player unless we own his rights. So, I want to draft Barry very late even though he isn't signable, and then work with him through the summer before he goes off to college and we lose his rights." Craig had pitched up to Double-A ball years earlier in the pros before handing in his glove to become a scout.

Dad was pleased and responded, "Craig, you've got a deal." Just like those banana nut muffins at Costco, my father once again got his cake and ate it too. The plan was for me to go to the University of California at Santa Barbara in a few months but receive some free professional pitching instruction while also being on the radar of a major league team.

Transforming My Form

So on June 5, 1996, just after graduation, the Seattle Mariners picked me in the fifty-ninth round of the major league draft. In that day, there was no actual limit on draft rounds but today there is a cap at fifty. Just as he promised my dad, Craig and I began meeting on the practice mounds at Grossmont Junior College's baseball field.

This was the first private coaching I received since I had stopped working with Randy Jones.

The first thing Craig pointed out was that my arm slot was way too high. I was what coaches call an "over-the-top pitcher." He told me, "We have to get your delivery more compact. Your levers are way too long. Your arm slot needs to be lower so you can whip it faster. Your leg kick is too high and it's throwing you off-balance. You need to keep your limbs closer to you, so you can rotate your hips with more snap as you release the ball. All of your movements need to be smaller and more efficient."

In his first minute of dialogue, Craig rocked my world. What he was asking me to do was completely change the style I worked so hard to develop over the last eight years. Those first few lessons were *so* awkward for me. The adjustments felt *so* foreign. And I hated it.

Craig spotted another major flaw in my delivery. I was throwing *across* my body. Instead of stepping directly toward the plate with my right leg, I always stepped toward the first base dugout. As a result, I wasn't able to get my hips fully open and squared up to the plate. So Craig took a six-foot metal pole and laid one end on the rubber mound with the other end pointed down the slope toward home plate, creating a perfect centerline. I was accustomed to stepping about eighteen inches left of that pole, but now Craig wanted me to step all the way on the *other* side. I felt like I was lunging ten feet from my old landing spot while in reality it was less than two feet.

The purpose of the drill was to allow my hips to fully open toward the plate while my upper body was still closed, creating maximum torque for me to come unwound and throw the pitch. Craig told me the greater the separation of rotation between my lower and upper body, the more velocity I could have on the ball. His end goal for me was increasing speed on my fastball.

During that same summer before I started college, I played in

Palomino League, an amateur team of seventeen- and eighteen-year-olds. Our home games were at Blair Field at Long Beach State, and I drove two hours up there every week to play.

Craig came to Long Beach to watch me whenever he had the time. As I eventually began feeling more comfortable with my new compact delivery, after one of those games, he walked up and asked, "Hey Lefty, you know what you hit on the radar gun today?" Surprised, I answered, "No, no idea." Craig said, "87 mph." I freaked out. I couldn't believe I had picked up 5 mph in only two months. All of my hard work was paying off fast.

Back then, the average major league fastball was roughly 88 mph. Over the past twenty years, that speed has jumped up to almost 93 mph. Biomechanical analyses, sport-specific training programs, high-performance diets, and sports psychologists have all attributed to speeds becoming higher for today's pitchers.

Setting Records, Getting Attention

In September of 1996, I started my college baseball career at UC Santa Barbara. Toward the end of October, there was a special practice game called Scout's Day where professional scouts came to assess the school's new crop of players. In that game, I hit 90 mph for the first time. Getting to that number is a major threshold for any pitcher.

By January of 1997, I hit 93 mph in our first game of the season. I had gained 11 mph in only eight months, all thanks to Craig's change in my technique. Even though the Mariners no longer owned my rights, I felt a strong connection to him for the incredible way he helped me.

With the added velocity, my curveball got even better, becoming less of a big, looping pitch and more of a deceptive late-breaking one.

The best asset any pitcher can have is an arsenal where every pitch looks the same to the hitter until the last millisecond. My curveball was now looking more like a fastball when it came out of my hand until it dropped under the hitter's bat, just before crossing the plate.

On the first weekend of the season, we played at Arizona State, a nationally ranked team. I pitched in relief the first two games. That Friday and Saturday night, I set a collegiate record of most consecutive outs by strikeout at nine in a row.

There was a distinct difference in my performance once I started throwing at speeds in the nineties. I had much less time to see how the hitter reacted to my pitch. I was throwing so hard that the ball was already popping into the catcher's glove before I had time to look up after the release. For as long as I could remember, after I threw a ball I had all the time in the world to look up to see how the hitter reacted. Not anymore.

That Saturday night following the game after everyone had left but while the lights were still on, I ran poles (going from left foul pole to right foul pole and back) to wind down and get the lactic acid out of my body to decrease the soreness. I vividly recall the strong sense of satisfaction I had that night while Mom and Dad waited for me in the stands. I felt great about my performance, so therefore I felt good about myself.

For the first time in my life, I began to take inventory of my potential: I'm left-handed. I have a special curveball. And I'm throwing consistently in the nineties. I realized that night in Scottsdale, Arizona, that getting to the major leagues was a very real possibility. This wasn't one of Mom or Dad's positive affirmations, but my starting to see for myself my dream was actually achievable. The numbers don't lie. Stats are stats. The bottom line was if you were a left-handed pitcher throwing over 90 mph, major league teams were going to pay attention.

Two well-known amateur publications at that time, *Baseball*

America and *Collegiate Baseball*, released articles about me after those Arizona State games. One stated, "Barry Zito Sets NCAA Record at Nine Strikeouts in a Row with 93 MPH Pitches." After being in the bullpen the first couple of weeks of the season, the coaches gave me a starting role.

Also my teammates began to relate to me a little differently after that night. Throughout that season they made sly compliments like, "Z, you better not forget me when you're rich and famous one day."

In college, big games are always on the weekend. Tuesday and Thursday games aren't as important and are usually against lesser opponents. The best starter on the team throws on Friday night to set the tone for the three-game series. The number two guy starts on Saturday and the number three man on Sunday. I was promoted to the Sunday starter as a freshman. We were in the Big West Conference, the same as California State University Fullerton and Long Beach State, who were high-powered teams that often made it to the college World Series.

My stats ended up telling two different stories as I finished out the rest of that year as a starter. Going 3–6 with a 6.43 ERA, I allowed too many runs and didn't win many games. But if I wasn't giving up walks and home runs, I was striking guys out, racking up 123 that season, which was second to the all-time record at UCSB. In just eighty-five innings, I had the highest collegiate strikeout ratio in the country. I was striking out thirteen guys per every nine innings, which is how the stats are counted. As a result, I ended up making the freshman all-American team.

Because I was consistently throwing hard, my arm hurt all the time. I spent a lot of hours in the training room with my left shoulder on ice. No matter what, I continued working diligently on my delivery to keep improving. Around this same time, I started a new exercise while running poles. I did pitching windups instead, one at a time, rather than just running, slowly going from foul pole to foul pole, moving about five feet at a time with each delivery. The windows in the coaches' offices faced the field, and I wasn't sure if they were impressed with my dedication or thought I was crazy. Or maybe a little of both?

Long Toss Method

Dad's training routines permanently infiltrated me because when I practiced in the bullpen, I set up my camcorder on a tripod to record every pitch. My family gave me a new digital model, the first recorder with the flip-out monitor. The new technology allowed me to watch my delivery frame by frame directly from the small playback screen straight off the camera. After throwing a couple of pitches, I watched my delivery to analyze my form. I then made the necessary adjustments on the next few pitches. At college, I duplicated by myself everything I had done with my dad in the backyard.

I still talked to Dad three or four times a week on the landline in my dorm, and he and Mom often drove the four hours north to the home games I pitched. Since we played along the West Coast, they traveled anywhere they could to see me play. While Dad never talked about his feelings of not working together anymore, there must have been a major void in his life because we were no longer hanging out in the backyard every day.

But to no one's surprise, Joe Zito figured out a new way to adapt and attack. He shifted from pitching coach to talent manager, engaging and building a network of specialists for my future. For example, as my skills were steadily increasing as a pitcher, Dad began to realize I needed a higher profile school. But he also knew how much I had established a great life in Santa Barbara, where I had good friends and was able to go to the beach whenever I could.

Dad found a guy in Los Angeles named Alan Jaeger who had

written a few articles about injury prevention for pitchers' arms. He was an advocate of "long toss," which is a long-distance (three hundred feet) throwing routine. Alan also utilized arm circles and rehab-style elastic tubing meant to be implemented daily right before picking up a ball to throw. The "warm up to throw, don't throw to warm up" approach was new at the time.

Long toss is a very polarizing subject in baseball. For example, there were many pro teams that wouldn't allow players to throw a ball more than one hundred twenty feet until they got to the big league level. But there were other teams that encouraged throws up to three hundred feet. Coaches tended to fall on one side or the other on the subject.

So at the end of my freshman year season, Dad once again performed his magic and arranged for Jaeger to drive up and meet me at Santa Barbara City College. Mom and Dad came to the lesson too. Alan first showed me all the exercises with the arm circles and the tubing. Then he showed me his long toss method.

As a pitcher, three hundred feet felt foreign at first because I never had to throw anywhere near that far. After taking time to warm up and gradually increase the distance, Alan had me back up toward the left field foul pole as he was stationed at home plate. I had to take a two-step crow hop to get momentum and then throw the ball along a huge arc as far as I could. Once I worked my way back in to regular catch distance, Alan told me to visualize that I was still making that long three-hundred-foot throw, but to just hold on to the baseball a split second longer. The goal was to create more freedom and looseness in my delivery. As a result, the pitches seemed to burn into his glove far more powerfully than before.

Dad knew my arm was hurting all the time, so *his* real goal with Alan was to help me find ways to sustain my performance while avoiding injury. My shoulder did not like the stress I was putting it through at UCSB. Even though I now had a big league fastball,

I was in danger of creating an injury that could jeopardize my big league dreams.

After my initial training with Jaeger was finished, I went to the Cape Cod summer league, playing with, and against, the top players in college baseball. That was also my first wood bat league, so I was able to get a taste of play in pro ball. That summer in the Cape, our team had an amazing season, won the 1997 championship, and as a result, even more attention started coming my way.

The Next Level

After I came back to California, started the fall quarter in Santa Barbara, and was playing fall ball, Dad began plotting the next phase of my career. He contacted Dennis Gilbert, one of the top sports agents at the time. Dennis had started Beverly Hills Sports Council and represented huge talent like Mike Piazza, Barry Bonds, and the flashy football player Brian "The Boz" Bosworth. To this day, I have no idea how my father got Dennis's attention, because he was just another dad with a kid playing college ball. So when he told me we were going to be on a conference call with Dennis Gilbert, I was instantly intimidated.

Unbeknownst to me, Dad and Dennis had already discussed my career, so the whole thing was a bit of a premeditated setup. But Dad knew I would be more open to Dennis's advice than his, especially if it meant having to leave my life by the beach. So on the call that November, Dennis said to me, "Look, Barry, if getting to the big leagues is your ultimate goal, you need to leave Santa Barbara and play for a junior college so you can get drafted sooner than later. I am certain this will be the best move for your career."

The rule to which Dennis was referring was once you start college at a four-year school, you have to play at least three years until you become draft eligible. But if you are at a junior college, you can be drafted after each season. I listened intently and was polite to Dennis, but when we got off the phone, I told Dad, "No! I don't want to leave. I want to stay in Santa Barbara and enjoy my life. It's so beautiful here. I love my friends and I love my team."

But as you are now on the inside of my life and know enough about the relationship, you can guess how this story ended. Yep, Dad swayed me. He always said things to try and convince me, like, "Barry, I am not smarter or wiser, I just have fifty years on you."

So two weeks before Christmas break, I walked in unannounced to my coach's office. Nervously, I sat down across from his desk and blurted out, "Hey Coach, uh, I'm thinking about transferring to a different school, a junior college in LA."

The very last thing he expected me to say and also the worst possible thing I could have said to him, I had uttered in a single sentence. I was his star player and was going to be his number one starter on Friday nights for the upcoming spring season. To him, that deal was sealed.

But essentially, my coach's head exploded. I watched the shock hit, the red rise up from his neck to his face, and then his eyes bulge out. He began to fidget nervously and talk very fast, managing to get out a few nouns and verbs in between the long string of curse words. He went off on me—*Off* with a capital O.

As his spit was flying my way, feelings of guilt began to set in. I was overcome with the sense of betrayal that I was stepping out on my coach and my team for the upcoming season. In an effort to alleviate my regret and his rage, I muttered, "Okay, Coach, well, let me go back and talk to my dad." When I got to my apartment, I immediately called home.

When my father answered, I told him, "Dad, Coach went nuts when I told him I wanted out. I think this is the wrong decision." I was secretly happy that the coach reacted the way he did because that gave me more leverage to convince my dad to let me stay. I said whatever I could to change his mind. Listening in by his side, Mom just wanted me to be happy, so she was supportive of my plea.

Once I got home for Christmas break, the three of us talked and all agreed for me to start *and* finish the season at Santa Barbara. Dad made it clear to us that he was going against his business instincts to see me happy. But I'm sure my coach was convinced his rant had been what persuaded me to stay, while Dad was just biding his sweet time.

I truly had a dream life at UCSB. I had picked up surfing in San Diego a few summers earlier before attending college, so returning to school in January, I got in some great rides at Sands Beach, the campus spot where all the students went to surf. There were some big winter swells that hit the central coast that year. I became part of the thriving surfing culture in Santa Barbara, was the star pitcher, and had good friends.

Heading South on the 101

Although he agreed to let me stay at Santa Barbara, since Dad couldn't deliver on his promise, he began focusing once again on my long-term baseball career, not just college. After only a couple of weeks back at school, he started reminding me of all the advantages of going to a junior college in LA. He never failed to mention that he was just holding me accountable to the dream I had since I was a kid.

Although I was still resisting, Dad was wearing me down. Even though I just wanted to be a normal college kid, I knew he was right. If Santa Barbara wasn't serving my ultimate career goals, there was no point in staying. Finally after much discussion, the unanimous decision was made for me to transfer to Pierce Junior College in LA, following my year and a half at Santa Barbara.

To avoid another conflict with the coach or anyone on the team, Dad came up with a covert plan. A few days after we decided to transfer, my parents rented a large cargo van and were parked and waiting at my apartment when I returned from practice. We packed up all my stuff and hit the road. The last stop before heading south was Caesar Uyesaka Stadium where I had just finished practice hours earlier.

Knowing the players and coaches were gone, I crept into our home locker room, went up to number forty-one, and cleared out my things. Then we hit the road to Los Angeles, executing our plan to position my career the best way possible to one day find big league stardom.

Ridden with guilt from stepping out on my baseball brothers, just weeks before the season began, I vowed never to show my face at that field again. Although "Baseball Barry" was excited about getting pro ball attention, the other side of me was angry and confused about the whole situation.

But whenever I began doubting the decision to transfer schools, I often heard Dad's voice in my head reminding me, "Barry, if you truly want to be a great champion, great sacrifice is required."

4

Method to the Madness

"I'm going to be in this game for a long time. I want to make my mark."

—My interview in *Esquire*[1]

Hey, this is Joe Zito. We're just letting you know that Barry will not be attending your school any longer. We just drove into Los Angeles and he will be enrolling tomorrow at LA Pierce Junior College and will pitch for them this year. Thanks for everything!"

Sitting in the car with the windows rolled down, Mom and I overheard Dad as he spoke into the gas station pay phone leaving that message for the athletic director at the University of California at Santa Barbara. Once we got to LA, we pulled off the highway at around eight o'clock that evening for him to make the call.

Later, I spoke with one of my teammates from Santa Barbara who told me, "When we all showed up the next day for practice and saw your locker had been emptied out, I knew exactly what you did and why you did it." I also heard later through the grapevine that, coming as no surprise to anyone, my coach was furious with me for sneaking out. But years later, he invited me back to play in an alumni game, which I took as a gesture of his forgiveness.

Unable to pay for my housing in LA, Dad had set up an arrangement with my new baseball coach at Pierce for me to live with one of the players and his single mother. The problem no one knew at the time was that she was a recovering heroin addict who created a very unpredictable environment. I went from life by the beach with close friends to staying with two strangers in the San Fernando Valley.

After my first week in the strange house, I composed a letter to all my closest friends back in Santa Barbara. I explained how I had to leave school because it was better for my baseball career, but that I really just wanted to be back at the beach with them. As I was writing, my tears fell onto the page, smudging the words. I felt like my baseball career was holding me captive in a part of the world where I hadn't chosen to live. To make matters worse, just a few days later, I found bent, burnt spoons in the drawers. I knew that meant my host mom was using again, which created even more turbulence in my new "home."

When I could get a day or two free, I often drove my brown 1979 Volkswagen Dasher, an old, highly uncool station wagon with a diesel engine, back up the coast to Santa Barbara to reconnect with everyone I missed so badly. On the return trip to LA, I always got really nervous driving up the Conejo Grade, a very steep four-mile section of the 101 highway. As I approached, I got into the far right lane, sometimes on the shoulder, and dropped the VW down into second gear. Then I prayed my way up the hill at a top speed of twenty-five miles an hour. The fact that my over-revved motor never went up in flames was a miracle. I will never forget the sputtering of that diesel engine getting loud enough to drown out my music on the radio.

As always, for the sake of baseball, I just toughed it out and didn't complain to anyone. But eventually, my coach got wind of the woman's drug addiction and moved me to another player's home. The other guy's mom and dad were awesome, and the healthier environment allowed me to focus on the field.

I made a great connection with my pitching coach at LA Pierce. We had a solid season and won our conference, going to the playoffs, but losing out before we could get to the California Junior College World Series. I had a good season for the Brahmas, racking up as many as seventeen strikeouts in some games. I was continuing to improve and felt I was getting closer and closer to my dream of playing professional baseball.

Like You Got Nothin' to Lose

Since the Seattle Mariners were forced by the rules of major league baseball to give up their rights to me once I started school at UC Santa Barbara, I had no ties to any pro team. One of the main reasons my father chose a junior college in Los Angeles was that all of the LA-based scouts could easily come watch me pitch. Every time I took the mound at Pierce there were large groups of scouts clustered behind the backstop with their radar guns pointing my direction.

Being draft eligible at Pierce, scouts again began to inquire as to how signable I was. Dad told them all, "We want to go in the first or second round but if we don't, we want first- or second-round money. If that doesn't happen, we'll head back to a four-year school and go in the first round next year." Once again, they were all working to not eye roll and responded with a patronizing, "Okay, sure, Joe."

As draft day approached, I was invited to throw bullpens for several pro teams. The most memorable time was in San Diego at Qualcomm Stadium, the home of the Padres, when I got to walk out on the same field where I had watched them play my entire childhood. I threw a nerve-racking bullpen while the Padres' general manager Kevin Towers stood right behind me, gauging my talent himself. Afterward, he said that if the Padres were to take me, they would use their ninth pick in the third round.

But when the draft came, the Padres passed on me. Honestly, that broke my heart because being chosen by my home team would have been such a cool experience. And maybe one day, I'd even play alongside my hero, Tony Gwynn. However, the Texas Rangers called my name with the very next pick, the tenth in the third round. I was just twenty years old and now a top-five-round pick! All those many years of hard work felt worth the effort and this was the moment for which Dad and I had sacrificed so much.

Then the negotiations for my signing bonus began. Average money that year for my draft position was around $300,000. The Rangers offered $250,000. Even with my family under such financial strain, Dad came back with, "Give us $350,000 and Barry is yours."

Finally, at $287,500, they told us, "That's it. That's all we can do. Take it or leave it."

We had a few days to let the team know our decision. I wanted so badly to sign the contract and head out to A-Ball Pulaski, Virginia, where I could begin my pro career and climb the ranks to pitch one day for the Texas Rangers. Not only was the baseball side exciting, but also the big money could give me the cash to buy my dream car—a black Dodge Durango. I had a poster of one taped up in my room. If I signed the dotted line, I could go to the dealership and pay cash.

But Dad didn't let up, explaining, "Barry, I know you think it's best for you to go play pro ball right now but you have got to trust me. You are capable of so much more, of being a first-round pick."

"But Dad, I don't care about the first round. I just wanna go play!"

Patient, but firm, he responded, "Barry, I'll say it again. I am not smarter than you; I just have fifty years on you. This is the right decision."

Like I did every time over the years, I gave up the fight. Because of Dad's solid track record making my career decisions, I was beginning to feel incapable of trusting my own instincts. So even though a quarter of a million dollars was life-changing money, my father knew better.

Dad responded to the Rangers, "Cape Cod summer league starts in two weeks. You have until then to sign Barry for $350,000. Once he is wearing a Cape Cod uniform, that price goes up to $500,000. When he comes home, you can sign him for $750,000 before he heads back to school."

The Rangers declined with no further discussion. Clearly, nothing was going to happen that year.

Living in the Jailhouse

Back when I was a freshman at Santa Barbara, my mom called me one night and said that they were having a really hard time financially and had to move out of my childhood home into a nine-hundred-square-foot duplex in the rough East Madison neighborhood of El Cajon. She told me that when I came home to see them, I would no longer have a bedroom. I was of course sympathetic to their plight, but still a bit stunned that when I visited, I'd have to sleep on the couch in my own home.

The place my parents rented in El Cajon was around a century old and had originally been a women's jail, so the framing inside the walls was not wood but metal. There was just an old window-mounted AC unit for the entire house, so with 110-degree heat in the summer, needless to say, living inside that box was miserable. My family was in one half of the home, and the owner lived on the other side, an older gentleman who had converted the house. When I came home, knowing I didn't have my own room, he agreed to give up one of his unit's bedrooms for me. He even relocated the dead bolt on the door that separated his side from ours.

With my pitching performance in the Cape, all the big schools that I only dreamed of attending were interested in recruiting me for the upcoming 1999 season. I always wanted to go to Clemson because Kris Benson went there. He was the first pick in the country in 1996 when I was a senior in high school. I had constantly watched videos of Kris pitching to dissect his delivery, trying to copy his every move. He wore number 34 because of Nolan Ryan, but I wore that number all through college because of Kris.

Being able to have my pick of virtually any Division 1 program, I told Dad I wanted to go to Clemson or the University of Southern California (USC). He agreed. With Clemson on the other side of the country, I signed a letter of intent with nearby USC.

When we returned home from the Cape, the plan was for me to attend a local junior college for the fall 1998 semester. I could earn my AA degree, which was necessary according to the NCAA four-two-four rule, and become eligible to return to a four-year university the following spring to play ball. So there were Dad, Mom, and me living in the tiny converted metal-frame "jailhouse" duplex for several months while I went to school.

When my sister Sally was just twenty years old, she had made the brave call to try and attend Berklee College of Music. With not even an application submitted, she bought a bus ticket to Boston and went there with literally nothing. She arrived at the prestigious school, managed to get an audition, and not only got accepted but took out school loans and worked full-time to stay afloat. On top of all that, she managed to send money back to Mom and Dad, who were in dire straits financially. Six years later, Sally graduated after putting herself through school single-handedly. Around the same time I moved home, Sally had also decided to come back to start her music career in California.

So as two adults both starting new chapters in our lives, my sister and I were sharing a room in this horribly hot house, each on our own twin mattress. Suzy, the Dalmatian dog I grew up with, slept on her dog bed in our room, too, mostly because Mom didn't want "that flea bag" anywhere else in her house. Sally and I always joked that the ceiling fan did nothing but blow the flea eggs off the dog and onto our beds and clothes that hung in the nearby open closet. Sally was twenty-nine and I was twenty, and Dad gave each of us the same weekly allowance of twenty dollars. Once a week, we packed up Mom's wood-paneled Datsun station wagon with all our dirty clothes to head down to the local laundromat and feed quarters in to wash clothes. We were poor by anyone's standards, even using food stamps to get groceries.

I had developed an aggravating issue with my knee that had gotten worse during my season at Pierce. The injury originated from a stupid stunt I had pulled with my friends that involved my riding on the hood of a moving car when I was sixteen. I finally went to a doctor, and after an X-ray, he told me I had a piece of dead bone that was going to cause a problem down the road for my career. I could feel the sting in my left leg every time I pushed off the mound.

With surgery the only remedy, I decided I had better take care of the problem during that off-season fall semester. I needed to be fully recovered and ready for my upcoming season at USC. My surgeon was Dr. Daly, who worked with the LA Clippers. My parents borrowed the $1,500 for the operation from friends.

So following surgery in the fall of 1998, I went to class by day and rehabbed my knee at night. To keep my delivery sound, I did my regimen of drills each evening in my parents' front yard. That semester was the slowest and simplest my life had ever been. But I was okay with the rest because I knew everything was about to change soon enough.

Being able to focus on school like I never had before resulted in my highest grades ever, earning a 4.0 GPA. I realized that if I applied myself fully, I could do well academically. I always loved science and math, and that semester I had a chance to actually excel in both.

Becoming a Trojan

With my first semester at USC about to begin, I moved into student housing just north of the South Central LA campus. My roommate was a German foreign exchange student. Yet again, I was not in a great part of town as my apartment had "burglar bars" on the doors and windows. Not only did I have a full-ride scholarship but I also received a special student athlete grant that allowed me to have a little spending money.

I *loved* playing for USC under legendary coach Mike Gillespie with John Savage as my pitching coach. John later became the head coach at UCLA. He ran us hard at the field every day, so my legs were so sore that I could barely walk to the bathroom in the middle of the night.

Dick Mills had introduced me to the concept of what he called "anchors." These were positive messages you put on the walls so you regularly see them. With my parents being into metaphysical spiritual elements, this kind of mental and emotional reinforcement was normal to me. So that first semester at USC in my room, I had messages like "15–0 Win/Loss Record" and "1st pick in the 1st round of the 1999 draft." Every night I lay there, staring up at those messages to stay motivated through the soreness.

As a result of feeling insecure around girls and, of course, with baseball being my first love, I never dated much at all. In the world-class training room at USC, I noticed this girl named Sophie who I knew was also very committed to her sport. She and I started talking and then hanging out. Before long, we began dating exclusively. I now had my first real relationship.

Ever since the previous fall when I signed my letter of intent, I had been looking forward to my first start with USC. That opening weekend, we traveled to the University of Texas at Austin, a major sports school. But all my anchors, positive messages, and inspiring thoughts didn't work that first game. As the new number one starter, I put too much pressure on myself to impress the team and pitched terribly. UT won all three games in that series.

After the rough opener, our team went on to have a great season. I contributed to the success in my starts, striking out up to sixteen hitters multiple times. I pitched one game at Washington State that had several weather delays from snow and a windchill of nine degrees. Regardless, I threw 154 pitches and struck out fourteen guys in a complete game victory.

Coping with Contradiction

While I was at USC, my mom became ill. Her skin had felt itchy and prickly for years, but that was only the beginning. After my first few starts, Mom's condition grew worse and she couldn't make it to any more of my games that year. Her skin turned orange-yellow and even the whites of her eyes became a mustard color. She was obviously jaundiced, but because my parents couldn't afford quality health care, Mom never got any solid answers from doctors.

Toward the end of my junior year season, she started retaining fluid in her limbs and swelling to the point that she actually began "leaking" a clear liquid from her wrists and ankles. She even strapped diapers to those areas to absorb the fluid. While she was visiting Sally one weekend after my sister had moved to LA, Mom was having such a hard time breathing that Sally insisted on taking her to the ER. Cedars-Sinai Medical Center was the closest, and upon observing Mom's condition, the doctors immediately admitted her. Finally, after running a barrage of tests, they diagnosed her with primary biliary cirrhosis, a liver disease unrelated to alcohol.

Mom's health continued to plummet just as I was reaching the heights of success I'd always dreamed of. I ended what had been an incredible season with the Trojans at 12–3. I was selected as a first team all-American and won the honor of Pac-10 Pitcher of the Year.

Our team sailed through the first round of the playoffs and headed north to Palo Alto to square up against Stanford. The winner of the three-game superregional series would go to the College World Series in Omaha, Nebraska. Dropping the Friday night game, I was to start on Saturday evening to try and save our chances of winning the series.

Unbeknownst to me, the Oakland A's sent all their brass to watch my performance. General manager Billy Beane, their scouting director, and other decision makers looked on as I pitched an awesome game. Although we lost 1–0, I only gave up two hits. The lone run that crossed the plate was a result of a fly ball getting lost in the dusky sky by our center fielder. My performance in that game won over the A's management.

With my dominating season coming to a close, I had positioned myself the best I could for the baseball draft that was now less than a week away. All the while, Mom was in the hospital fighting for her life. Knowing that a new liver was her only hope, the doctors put her on a transplant list. Because of her condition, her body was no longer clearing out the toxins, so they began to back up into her system, eventually working their way into her brain.

During one of my routine visits to see Mom, Sally pulled me aside in the hall and warned, "Barry, be prepared. She is not the mom we know right now." Even with the heads-up, I wasn't ready for what happened when I entered her room. Mom was delirious. She was slurring her words and blurting out things I couldn't understand. I approached her, looked right into her eyes, and said, "Mom, it's me! Bear!" But she wasn't there, like something had taken over her body. She even tried to stand on a rolling food-tray table before I forced her back down. The nurses had to come in and restrain her so she couldn't harm herself. Finally, they administered a drug that slowly returned her to a normal state of mind, even though she was still dying.

After having my best season yet in baseball, falling in love with a great girl who was an awesome athlete, and awaiting the pro draft with a very promising future, I was having an amazing year. But my mom was dying in the hospital. The tension was pulling me in opposite directions. I didn't know what to feel. Dad knew I was struggling and told me about an old Cole Porter song, "Down in the Depths on the Ninetieth Floor." The lyrics explained everything I was feeling—one part of your life going up exactly the way you always wanted, while at the same time, another part spiraling down-ward and falling apart.

When a Plan Comes Together

Finally, draft day arrived on June 2, 1999. Back then the pro draft was a conference call that you could listen in on. Mom and Sally were on the call from the hospital, and Bonnie was on from her home in San Diego. Dad and I were at my apartment at USC. Each team had only a minute or two to make their selection. I was so excited to potentially hear my name in the first round that the antic-ipation felt like electricity running through my body. The chances of everything coming together were far better than the previous year when the Rangers had come to the table.

We heard from scouts that the Rockies were highly interested at pick fifteen as well as the White Sox at twenty-two and of course the A's at number nine. I had an inkling I might go in the top fifteen picks but so much of what you hear from scouts around draft time is only hearsay, so nothing was certain.

As my family was waiting silently on the call, the pinnacle moment of my life had finally arrived. Each of the first eight teams chose their guy. Then the A's were up. We heard, "This is general manager Billy Beane. With the ninth pick, the Oakland A's select left-handed pitcher Barry Zito out of the University of Southern California."

Dad and I went crazy! Mom and Sally were going nuts in the hospital room. Bonnie was hooting and hollering. Everything went down *exactly* as planned. The A's offered $1.59 million as a signing bonus. That's 1,590,000—as in dollars.

Regardless of what anyone else may have thought along the way, Dad was dead-on in his strategy. Those many years of planning and predictions had materialized just like he said.

I wonder how many of those scouts and coaches over the years heard about me and the money, and thought, "Well, I'll be darned. Joe Zito *was* right. His son was a top-ten pick in the first round, and they got the big numbers he said they would get. Good for them."

Barry's Basics—Second Base

M any people aren't aware that the level of baseball they watch on national TV is the highest of seven professional levels. When a pro team drafts a player out of either high school or college, he goes directly into a feeder system from which the major league team can pull players. Lower minor league levels are strictly for player development, while upper levels are for supplying viable talent to the big league squads.

Minor League Levels

Each level of the minors has roughly two leagues. Usually one is on the west side of the country and the other on the east side. The multi-tiered "farm system" is laid out like this:

- *Rookie Ball:* Mostly adolescent international players and high school draftees, where the season is only three months long at around seventy-six games.
- *Short Season A:* Like Rookie Ball, but with better talent. Standout high school players and many college players start here.

- *Low-A Ball:* Full baseball season of about 140 games. Standout college players often begin their professional careers here.
- *High-A Ball:* Only reached after ascending the other ranks, unless an elite college player is assigned here, which is rare.
- *Double-A Ball:* Attained after a few years in the minor leagues and where you begin to encounter players with "major league tools," such as pitchers who can throw both hard and accurate, and hitters that can not only make consistent contact with the ball but also hit home runs.
- *Triple-A Ball:* Full of refined baseball talent and the last stop before the major leagues.

Getting Called Up

No matter which level a player is called up from, the process is generally the same. The general manager at the major league level oversees everything, from the big leagues on down to rookie ball. He communicates with the head of the minor leagues, called the director of player development. The director knows exactly which players are outperforming their current level and are ready to be called up.

Some organizations will give their big prospects a full season at each level to ensure that player is adjusting not only physically but also mentally as the competition gets better. If a player is moved through the system too quickly and he begins to struggle, the team is putting their coveted prospect at risk of losing his confidence, which might derail his career.

On the contrary, teams like the Oakland A's will move a prospect once that player shows he is ready for better competition, regardless of how quickly that may happen. This is the reason I got moved up at the pace I did. If I had been with a different organization, I might have stayed in A-Ball for my entire first season and Double-A for the next season, seriously delaying my big league experience.

In the major leagues, there is a twenty-five-man roster. On September 1, teams can expand the roster to forty, thus the term, "September call-ups." Teams that are in a playoff race may not use the call-ups for anything other than an insurance buffer, in case someone gets hurt. But all the other teams who are out of the running use this part of the season to allow their up-and-coming talent to get in some big league time. Those games offer a taste of playing at the highest level without the normal pressure. Or at least not as much as there would be when chasing a world championship.

But in Triple-A, you have career players who stay there for many years, with some guys earning over six figures annually. Even though no one will ever hear of them, they make a great living for their families. Yet those players still live in the hope that maybe one day they'll get called up to the major leagues where the big money and fame are waiting. Regardless, those veteran players keep their minor league teams afloat. They also offer great competition to the prospects that are on their way up. Big league teams can invite whomever they want to spring training but will always have to cut the roster down to twenty-five before the season starts. So, many of those career minor leaguers go to big league camp every year but play out their seasons in Triple-A.

Occasionally when a major leaguer gets hurt, one of those guys will get called up to fill in for a few games. The forty-man roster contains the total pool of players eligible to be on the twenty-five-man roster in the majors. If the general manager wants to call a player up, he has to be on the forty-man roster first.

If the team wants to call a player up who isn't on the forty-man to fill a short-term need, they must first remove another player from that roster to make room, usually a player the organization highly values. Once this happens, the player that was taken off the forty-man is now free to get picked up by any of the other twenty-nine teams in baseball. This is the waiver process. If another team claims him off waivers, his old team loses him indefinitely. This is essentially why the career Triple-A players don't get called up, because the organization risks losing a player they value long-term.

As you can see, strategic management of the forty-man roster is critical to every team.

At Least Now We're in the Building

"I had a long talk with Barry and told him this is not about money. It's about nothing more than legacy."

—Joe Zito, *New York Times*[1]

B onus baby."

That was the label I wore entering professional baseball. It's the buzzword for a guy coming into the minor leagues with a hefty signing bonus. Word gets around fast when a high draft pick is coming to a team.

Having a guarantee of over a million dollars to sign was obviously far more than the few thousand bucks most of the guys in that league were given. Most players scraped by on the $700 a month standard salary for A-Ball players at that time. Fans have no idea that most of the minor league players are living paycheck to paycheck unless they do get some big money up front.

There's often an element of jealousy by opposing players *and* even your own teammates when a guy gets paid as much as I did to sign his pro contract. The bigger the money, the greater the expectation, and then they watch your every move all the more to see if you're "legit," meaning worth the hefty signing bonus.

Coming into the A's organization, they told me I was going to skip the two lower levels of A-Ball and go straight into High-A. The jump wasn't much of a stretch for me since I was coming out of the highly competitive Pac-10 Conference.

In 1999, Oakland's A-Ball team was the Visalia Oaks in the California League. The drive to the quaint little farming town was only a few hours north of Los Angeles. My car at the time was a 1989 Honda. The bumper was falling off so I had secured it with an old telephone wire. Most players are far from home, so I was really happy I could stay in my home state. On our off days, I was able to go visit Mom in the hospital.

Since I was a high-profile first pick, the Visalia players expected me to be a "dig me guy," which is ballplayer slang for self-absorbed. But I think I surprised them with my laid-back surfer mentality. Because of my personality and attitude, my teammates quickly accepted me as one of their own. I really tried not to behave like an entitled first rounder as so many do. In keeping with baseball tradition, one of the older players took me out that first week to the local bar, El Presidente, and made sure I drank way too much tequila.

A Surreal Six Figures

Even though I was a bonus baby, I still hadn't seen a single dollar because the huge checks take about six to eight weeks to be processed. Finally one day when I was in the barely-high-school-quality locker room in Modesto, our trainer was handing out the usual sealed envelopes with our paychecks. But when he got to me, he had a second envelope.

As he handed me both, he said, "I think that's the big one, Z."

"You mean my signing bonus?" I asked.

Lowering his voice a bit, he answered, "Yep, you may want to keep that one on you today."

I walked into the showers so I could be alone and tore into the envelope. My eyes quickly jumped to the right side of the check where I saw the really long number: $795,000. That moment was totally surreal. My mind immediately flashed back to all the dedication and struggles my family had gone through to give me the best chance for success in baseball, thinking to myself, *Mom and Dad's investment just paid off in a huge way!* I quickly began thinking of ways I could help my family and all the cool things I could buy that I always wanted but could *never* afford. And the really crazy part was that amount was only *half* of my bonus; another identical check was coming six months later.

Dad had already talked with Paul Cohen, my agent at the time, and started planning for the arrival of my first check. Paul connected him with a financial team to handle the money and begin to invest for us. My parents had amassed quite a bit of debt over the years, so the first thing we did was pay off *all* their bills.

I took great pride in helping my parents attain financial freedom after all their sacrifices. But as for me, being twenty-one, the next thing on the list was my dream car. The picture I had cut out and put on the wall in my "jailhouse" bedroom in San Diego was finally about to become a reality. My agent connected me to his "car guy" in Vegas, and I promptly ordered a new 1999 Dodge Durango, black with chrome rims, dark window tint, custom sound system, and a beefy, matte black grille with floodlights on the front. What an amazing ride! I got rid of the old Honda but kept the phone cord from the bumper.

Because Dad needed to be in LA full-time, close to Mom in the hospital, I rented a house for them in Encino and set them up with a monthly stipend for living expenses. So Dad got settled only twenty miles from Cedars-Sinai in Beverly Hills. If Mom ever got better and was able to go home, they still needed to be close to her doctors.

Another baseball dream came true for me soon after the big

check arrived. When you sign a pro sports contract, you give full permission to Major League organizations to use your likeness for their income streams. As a high draft pick, I showed promise to likely go on to the majors, which earned my first baseball card release. The photo on the front was snapped while I was pitching on the mound for the Visalia Oaks, releasing the baseball in the solid form I had learned years before from Craig Weissmann. On the back of the card was a blurb about how good my season had been for the Trojans and how I showed real promise to one day become a major leaguer.

From Jean to Jan

While I was acclimating to my new life playing pro ball, Mom was placed on a liver transplant list. But before they could approve the operation, she had to be in good health otherwise. There was one scare where she was given twenty-four hours to live. Unconscious and on a breathing tube, her entire body was once again riddled with toxins. Upon hearing the news, I left my team and drove to LA. I vividly remember staring out an empty hallway window in the hospital pondering what life might be like without Mom and her constant love and support. But somehow her body still had enough fight left and she pulled through.

Upon rejoining the team, I couldn't shake my fears about Mom dying. Before games I tried to stay focused on pitching, but the heaviness of her failing health was always weighing me down. My best friend was slipping away. Between innings of my games, my mind wandered to the past, recalling moments I shared with my mom as a child: going to the movies and eating popcorn together, giving her back rubs to help her stress from working at the church, lying on her bed on Saturday mornings and just talking about anything for hours. If Dad represented the logic and practicality of working toward a dream, Mom was the softhearted nurturer who kept me sane through it all.

A few weeks later on July 11, 1999, while on a road trip with the team, I was staying near the team hotel in Oakdale, California, with the parents of one of my college buddies. As my friend's mom was cooking breakfast, the phone rang. After answering, she immediately handed the receiver to me. I heard my sister Sally say, "Barry, Mom is finally getting a liver! You need to get down here *now*!" I called the team and told them the news. Since I had no car there, I borrowed my friend's mother's Volvo station wagon and hit the road.

Six hours later when I walked into the hospital, Mom was already in surgery. For the next ten hours, Dad, Sally, Bonnie, a family friend, and I sat in the waiting room trading stories about Mom. We also prayed the only prayer I knew back then, which we called "spiritual mind treatments." So together, we all spoke treatments out loud, affirming my mom's complete recovery with her new liver.

Evidently when the surgeon opened Mom up, he realized she was far more compromised than they thought and did not want to "waste a good liver on her." But another doctor spoke up at that moment and disagreed, insisting that Mom was a fighter and the transplant could be successful. Thanks to that doctor speaking with such certainty, the surgeon proceeded with Mom's transplant.

Just sixteen hours earlier, a middle-aged woman in Orange County had an aneurysm and died immediately. Her name was Jan. Her husband later told us that just a couple of weeks before the sudden tragedy, she had sat up in bed one night, looked at him very intentionally, and said, "Honey, I want to be an organ donor. So if I die before you, I want you to promise that you'll donate my organs." Since Jan was in perfect health, her husband didn't know what to make of such an adamant request—until that horrible day only weeks later when he remembered what his wife had made him vow to her.

My mom's name was Roberta Jean Zito. Following the surgery

and after hearing the entire story from Jan's husband, Mom changed her middle name from Jean to Jan to honor the benefactor who *literally* saved her life through her own death.

And after my mother's transplant, I also made the decision to become an organ donor.

Eight Weeks to Triple-A

Even with the long road to recovery ahead of her, I knew Mom now had a second chance at life. The heaviness in my heart began to lift, and I dove full force back into baseball. After pitching in A-Ball for six weeks, one day on a road trip, the trainer approached me with a coy smile on his face and said, "Hey Z, I got some news for you."

Wide-eyed, I responded, "Yeah?"

He continued, "Lip just called. You're going up to Midland!" (Lip was Keith Lippman, director of player development.)

I couldn't believe it. After only six weeks in High-A, I was already heading to the upper levels of the minor leagues. I cheered my team on that game while daydreaming the entire time what Double-A might be like. So that night after the game, I got on a plane to meet the Midland RockHounds in El Paso on a road trip.

For the first time in my career I felt intimidated. This was Double-A. Serious baseball skill here. These guys were good. Like *really good*. The game was faster. The players were fully grown, *adult* men. I felt like a boy among them. While I had always thought the biggest skill-level jump in pro ball was between Triple-A and the majors, I learned by experience it was actually between Single-A and Double-A. Over the next three weeks, I didn't pitch well at all, only having one decent game.

Another aspect of pro ball that I did not see coming was the road trip sexual escapades that took place. One of my first nights with the team, we were staying in a hotel. I knew that my roommate was in a serious relationship with a girl back in his hometown. He asked me, "So you got a girlfriend?" With stars in my eyes, I said, "Yeah, dude, I am in love with a girl I started dating in college." He smirked and said, "Well, you'll learn." After our game, he didn't get back to our room until the wee hours of the night. He actually woke me up to tell me about the "hotty" he had met and went into detail about their "hookup."

Just a few hours later, the next morning, I overheard him talking to his girlfriend on the phone, lying to her about what he had done the night before. At this point in my life, I had only kissed a couple of girls. Hearing my teammate's story and realizing his double life made me really uncomfortable. After that night, I knew I was now living in a *very* different world.

On the final day of the Midland season, our manager, Tony DeFrancesco, called my hotel room. "Zito, you and Bert Snow are getting called up to Triple-A Vancouver. Tomorrow is the last day of their season and you'll be starting for them in Colorado Springs. Get your stuff packed and get to the airport."

Vancouver was going to the playoffs, but since a few of their pitchers were getting called up to the big leagues, they needed some roster help from Bert and me. In short, if Vancouver *wasn't* going to the playoffs, then I *wouldn't* have been called up.

So in that final game of the season in Colorado Springs, my coach told me, "Zito, these guys you're facing will be swinging first pitch. They aren't heading to the playoffs and just want to get out of here and go home. So just throw strikes." I pitched six innings, gave up only one run, and got the win.

Following that game, we returned to Vancouver for a few days before the playoffs started. Arriving from West Texas was a culture shock to say the least. There were actually some decent restaurants and places to go at night. As a general rule of thumb, the higher the level of ball, the better the city. While in Vancouver, I realized I was climbing up the baseball food chain.

I pitched well in the playoffs and we made it to the Triple-A World Series in Las Vegas. I remember when I saw Dave Hollins's name on the other team's lineup sheet before my big start. He was the first major league player I had seen on TV that I got to pitch against. In that moment I felt closer to "the bigs" than ever before. While I pitched an okay game, I got a lot of run support and we went on to win the whole thing. *My ring, please!*

Going from college ball straight into the minors, then after only eight weeks into my pro career being sent up to Triple-A, and then winning a championship was a whirlwind for me. At such an early stage of my pro career I felt grateful for everything that was happening. But at the same time I knew I was just fulfilling the baseball destiny my dad had always said was waiting for me. Although these were milestones, they felt more like checking boxes on my career to-do list. Nothing more than another few steps in a long climb up Joe Zito's pitching mountain. And I was nowhere near the summit by Dad's standards.

Three Chords and the Truth

In 1999, my sister Sally had been living by herself in a flat in Sycamore Park, a neighborhood in West Hollywood. So when I returned home from Vancouver, I moved in with her. Actor Michael Rapaport lived in our complex, and we routinely overheard him running his lines for the different characters he was playing. I remember that I felt so cool because I lived near movie stars, even though we were just in a nice apartment.

I was still dating Sophie, who was in her last year at USC, and I'd regularly make the half-hour drive down to South Central to see her. Her roommate Beth was supercool, and she was always singing while playing her acoustic guitar. Curious, I asked her if she could show me a few chords. Holding my fingers in those weird positions on the frets felt totally different from holding a baseball. But I was hooked.

After barely getting G, E minor, and D down on Beth's acoustic, I headed to Guitar Center on Sunset Boulevard and took home an Ovation Celebrity acoustic-electric, the popular model back then, with a plastic rounded back and a plug for an amp. The guitar became a permanent part of my life that winter.

My dad always had an aversion to my getting involved with music, warning, "Barry, in baseball you must only master three pitches. If you do that, you can write your own ticket in life. With music, however, it's about the machinery behind you and regardless of your talent, you will likely never make a living."

So I was obviously concerned to tell Dad about my new obsession with the guitar. I knew I had to assure him that I was still 100 percent committed to baseball. No matter what else came into my life, a girl or a surfboard or whatever, I had to convince him that it wouldn't take my focus off pitching.

When I finally worked up the nerve to tell Dad about the guitar, I explained that I needed a healthy distraction from baseball. The truth was, playing pro ball was beginning to feel like living in a fishbowl, and the guitar gave me something that was just mine and no one else's, not even Dad's. While I could tell he was concerned, he was supportive. And I was relieved.

So at twenty-one-years old, music found its way into my life after I had been raised all those years as a jock in a family of musicians. Most pro ballplayers spent their downtime playing golf or video games but I figured I could easily carry my guitar on road trips and start to develop a skill far more useful than making par or winning at Xbox.

Santa Barry

The last several Christmases had been bleak for our family. The Christmas where Sally and I had been living with our parents in the "jailhouse" had been really tough, even depressing. We had all gone to the Dollar Store to buy each other gifts. Our Christmas tree was a sad, crooked Charlie Brown model that looked more like a cut-off branch.

That first off-season, I had plenty of money in the bank, my own credit card, and Mom was recovering at home, so when Christmas came around, I decided to go *big* for the family. Because of flying so often on road trips with the team, I always loved looking through *SkyMall* magazine tucked away in the seat back. They had all the coolest stuff. Where else can you find a life-size Sasquatch statue for your garden or an end table that doubles as a dog crate? So awesome, right? Let's just say I went a little crazy on a massive *SkyMall* order for the Zito family Christmas.

I pulled up to my parents' house on Christmas Eve in that big, black Durango with the seats folded down holding the sixty-plus gifts. To savor *every* moment for around three hours on Christmas morning, we took our time watching each person open presents.

That first professional season created a major shift in our family dynamic: while both my sisters were doing very well for themselves, I had become the sole provider for my parents. I was happy to finally be able to help them, especially to allow Mom the freedom to stop working at the church and focus on her journey of recovery.

Big League Camp #1

The year 2000 brought my first pro spring training. I knew I had little chance of making the team, but I didn't care because I was going to be rubbing elbows with real major league players. Most twenty-two-year-olds in pro ball were in minor league camp at one of the five levels there. But as a first rounder from the previous year, I had a "big league camp invite" written into my contract. Coming off such a successful rookie season, I came in feeling confident, while still in awe of sharing a clubhouse with legit players.

I got to start one game on the road in Tucson against the White Sox. Frank Thomas, one of my childhood heroes, was in the lineup that day. Back home, I had his 1990 Leaf baseball card in one of those thick, plastic protective cases with the tiny jeweler screws. But now I was watching him step into the batter's box to face *me*.

I threw Frank a 2–2 fastball up and away, and he slapped it for a base hit up the middle. At first, I got mad and thought, *Oh crap! He got a hit!* But then reality came over me and I immediately changed my tune. *Oh man! Frank Thomas just hit one of* my *pitches!* That was definitely a defining moment for me. I ended up playing on the same team as Frank six years later.

About a week before camp ended, manager Art Howe called me into his office and said, "Hey, we love how hard you're working. Love what you're doing. We believe you can help our team, but since you just got drafted, we're sending you down to minor league camp, so go do your thing in Triple-A." I knew the major leagues was not an *if* but a *when*, so I had no problem with the reassignment. Being able to stay at big league camp for six weeks before getting sent down was a huge victory. I was grateful to stay that long.

Dangerous Distractions

I was assigned to the Triple-A team, a new affiliate deal with Sacramento, pitching for about a week before we broke camp. Construction issues delayed completion of the new stadium, so we had to start the season with a *seven-week* road trip. Triple-A rules stated that we had to fly out on the first flight of the day to our road trips. So after a night game we'd finally get to sleep around midnight and have to be up a few hours later to catch a flight out as early as 5:30 a.m. Then upon arrival in the new city, we'd head straight to the field to get ready for the game that evening. That was a grueling two months.

During the seven weeks out, we played in Oklahoma City, the home of the Texas Rangers' Triple-A team, in a smaller replica version of the Ballpark at Arlington. Before the game, I played catch with the stud lefty prospect Mark Mulder, the A's first rounder in the 1998 draft. I remember feeling an adrenaline rush from being in such a beautiful ballpark with such a talented throwing partner. Knowing I was considered a coveted prospect myself, I began to be self-aware of my own importance.

In Triple-A, there are five starting pitchers in each game: one is on the mound, two are in the dugout, and the other two are in street clothes in the stands behind home plate charting the hitters and checking speeds with the radar gun. During that series in Oklahoma, another starter and I were up in the stands, and there were two girls just a few rows in front of us. I was still dating Sophie exclusively at the time. The girls knew who we were and likely had sat there to try and meet players. We started talking and eventually flirting. At the end of the game, they suggested we meet up with them in Bricktown, a trendy area near the field. We agreed. So later after we cleaned up, we met the girls and had dinner and some drinks.

Afterward, we split up into couples. I went back to the girl's place and ended up staying there all night. Being allured by a pretty girl, I cheated on Sophie for the first time. The fear I felt back when my womanizer teammate was bragging about his philandering was gone, and I was now doing the same thing many players do while on the road. I wish I could say that mistake taught me a lesson; unfortunately, it was more like I broke a seal on a jar of something

I couldn't pour back in. That was just the beginning of a reckless pattern of behavior for me that lasted far too many years.

In high school, I had worked hard to get the popular girls to like me, but they never saw me as boyfriend material. And then finally when a really pretty girl asked me to her prom, at the after-party when her ex showed up, I realized that all along she was just using me to make him jealous. Now in pro ball, all that pent-up insecurity led me to have an "I'll show them" attitude. Those years of frustration with women caused me to become a loose cannon now that my baseball success seemed to serve as some kind of new superpower with women. I found the old saying was true: "Women love a man in uniform."

Having done all kinds of drugs in high school, I realized sex, power, and fame are entirely different highs. As with so many traveling entertainers, the pattern became different city, different girl, but the same high. There is most certainly a correlation in pro sports of dominating *on* and *off* the field. Ironically, off the field endeavors could often make a player perform better. If he had a good night with the ladies, he took that shot of confidence onto the field the next day, and if he had a great game on the field, he was even more confident the next night in the bar. A vicious cycle.

But the guys weren't the only guilty party because, as they say, "It takes two to tango." Most of the girls had their own motives of wanting to tell their friends they had hooked up with a pro ball player.

But I also witnessed the dark side of this dynamic on the road one time with a teammate who was married. Late that night, he brought a girl back to our room. I was pitching the next day and had been in bed asleep for a while. As part of my "no distractions" policy that Dad had instilled, I always walked the straight and narrow the night before I started.

I was awakened by the sound of the girl crying and heard my teammate telling her to go home. He had done his business and wanted her out. Under the impression that she was staying all night, she pleaded with him for as long as she could. I heard him insisting she leave. Through her tears, I could feel her heart breaking over the reality that she had just allowed herself to be used. As he called her a cab, she quickly gathered her clothes, got dressed, and left. Although I heard everything, the entire time I just pretended to be asleep.

During this season, with Mom still recovering from the transplant and us being all over the map to play, Dad was not at the games much, but I was plenty motivated on my own without his help. Finally, Raley Field was officially opened, giving our team an incredible facility with lots of hometown love, selling out the 15,000-seat stadium, even outdrawing the A's by several thousand most nights.

My Moment of Truth

In July of 2000, while we were playing against the Stars in Las Vegas, my manager approached me with a big smile on his face. "Zito, you're going to the big leagues." Every kid who plays baseball longs to hear those words one day. I looked at him with a huge grin and asked, "Are you serious?" He answered, "Yup. You're getting on a plane to Oakland tomorrow and starting against the Angels on Saturday." The Angels had some serious studs in their lineup like Mo Vaughn, Tim Salmon, Garret Anderson, and Darin Erstad.

I had just recently gotten my first cell phone, so I stepped out of the clubhouse and called Dad. That was such a huge moment for him and me. He told me that when we got off the phone, he was going to call everyone he knew and plan the caravan to drive up the next day to the game.

I felt an adrenaline surge like I had never felt before. Picturing myself going to the major leagues all those years was one thing, but the actual experience of getting called up was something exponentially greater. My self-worth and confidence instantly shot through the roof as I thought about being on TV soon, with kids across the country watching *me* pitch in the big leagues, just like I had done with my heroes years earlier.

But just before we hung up, Dad said, "Barry, we may be in the basement, but at least now we're in the building." Joe Zito always had a way of providing a sober reality of where I was and where I still had to go.

Ride That Wave

"I think I'm aware of what goes on in my mind more than some guys and for that reason I fight more battles."

—My interview in *Sports Illustrated*[1]

Hey, meat! What in the world is all that crap?"

"You got some b**** for a college kid!"

"Never seen that move before!"

Once Billy Taylor, the A's intimidating closer, started yelling insults and jabs at me, the other pitchers quickly joined in. Kind of like when the alpha wolf goes in for the kill, the others join in the frenzy and the blood starts to fly.

I was trying to focus, but also thinking, *Welcome to the big leagues, Zito.*

In 1999 when the A's drafted me, I flew to Oakland to throw a bullpen session for the big league pitching coach. I showed up in the middle of batting practice while all the A's players were out on the field. I went to the left field line to start my arm circles and tubing exercises like I always did to warm up. I noticed that, one by one, the veteran pitchers were watching me as they shagged fly balls in the outfield. I could tell by the way they were laughing and pointing that something bad was about to happen. When Taylor and the other guys started ragging me, I just did my best to ignore them and focus on pitching for the coach.

Fast-forward to the summer of 2000, and I was being called up to play for real with those same guys. I was eager for my debut and fired up that I had the chance to be in front of the Oakland fans. I caught my flight to the Bay and checked into the team hotel, the Airport Hilton. Around 8:00 p.m. that night, I went to the bar to watch the telecast of the game being played just a few miles away. Tim Hudson, the hottest young pitcher in the league, was starting the series opener against the Angels. He was having a really tough game, even taking a line drive off the chest that made me cringe. Knowing how good Huddy was and watching him struggle with Anaheim's lineup made the reality of what I was about to do start to sink in.

Ascending level by level in baseball for so many years, I had finally arrived at the last stop. I had to "rise to the occasion," as my father always said. I was going up against the best team I had ever faced but felt confident in my three pitches: fastball, curveball, and changeup. I didn't know what was going to happen in my game, but I knew I was going to leave everything on the field that day.

299 More to Go

The next morning, I walked into the Oakland A's clubhouse and was immediately greeted by Steve Vucinich, the clubhouse manager. A warmhearted man, he gave me a congratulatory hug and escorted me to my assigned locker, letting me know they had picked out number 53 for my jersey. While I was acting cool on the outside, on the inside I was overcome with a childlike excitement, thinking, *Holy smokes, I'm in the big leagues!*

The players were sitting around tables, playing cards, just like in the minors, but the surge of major league energy felt worlds apart from where I had been only days before. The food room looked like the inside of a convenience store, complete with every snack, candy bar, and beverage you could ever want. No more peanut butter and jelly sandwiches and bad coffee like in Triple-A.

Rick Peterson, the A's pitching coach, was the one guy throughout my career who really understood me. People in the game either loved Rick or hated him, because take it or leave it, he knew who he was and wasn't going to change for anyone. Rick was far more artistic and sensitive than the typical baseball personnel and that either scared people off or made them follow him without question. I was also a rare archetype in the game, doing yoga and reading philosophy daily. Something about us both being "different" led to an instant connection as player and coach.

Two years prior, back in 1998, my dad got in touch with Rick at his home in New Jersey when he was in between minor league baseball jobs. Always seeking out more pitching wisdom, Dad worked out a time for me to meet Rick in person once my Cape Cod summer season finished. Sally was in Boston at that time, so I stayed at her place for a few days after playing. One day, we hopped in her car and headed south for a long, rainy drive to Jersey. We pulled up to a parking lot where Dad arranged for Rick and me to meet. We talked pitching for thirty minutes in the rain, and I went through my delivery as he jotted down notes for me to take home and study.

Two years later, here we were: Rick was the A's pitching coach and I was the new hotshot rookie. Crazy, small world, and once again, Dad had orchestrated another masterpiece.

Before my big debut, Rick pulled up a chair to my locker, and in his always heartfelt, just-above-a-whisper voice asked, "Hey Z, how you doin' bud? Pretty cool, huh? You're in the big leagues." No one, and I mean *no one*, in pro sports does that kind of thing.

It's always just business as usual, never giving space for gratitude and awe of the game. Rick was the one and only coach who I felt actually saw me for *me*. In the pro sports world of testosterone-charged bravado, I always felt like I had to fit the rigid mold of being a "typical jock." So much so that I even changed my email one year to typicaljock@xxxx.com to remind me that I had to be more like the other guys in the locker room.

To this day, I believe 100 percent that the success I experienced in Oakland was to the credit of a coach that understood *who* I was. Rick never tried to get me to be someone or something I wasn't. In fact, if you look at my numbers those first four seasons with the A's, you'll see the indisputable evidence of our connection in my stats.

During a game in spring training when I was on the mound and not pitching well, Rick had called time-out. He walked to the mound with the simple goal of calming me down. Knowing my love for surfing, Rick asked, "You know how it feels to ride a wave, right?" I nodded. He continued, "Well, just ride the wave, Z." That's all he said, but the analogy made sense to me. I settled down and got my groove back.

In my major league debut versus the Angels, I had a 7–1 lead going into the fifth inning. I gave up a couple of base hits and a walk, getting myself into a no-outs, bases-loaded jam with the heart of the lineup approaching. Rick called time-out and jogged out to give me a breather. He walked up the mound and quietly asked, "How you doin', Z?" He put his hand on my back, leaned in, and continued, "Hey, remember field three in that spring training game earlier this year?"

I answered, "Yeah?"

Rick smiled and repeated his advice from months earlier. "It's just like riding a wave, Z."

My coach was just reminding me in *this* moment that even though I was in a big league game with the bases loaded and heavy hitters coming up, that same simple mind-set was still my path to victory.

Rick jogged back to the dugout, while I took a few deep breaths and relaxed, exactly how my coach had encouraged me to do. I then struck out the next three hitters in a row, stranding the runners on base and getting out of the inning untouched.

To bolster my confidence as a new major leaguer, my manager, Art Howe, had me warm up on the mound before the sixth inning, knowing full well my work was done for that day. He orchestrated the scene so that right before the hitter stepped in to begin the inning, he would take me out of the game so I could walk off the field and really soak up the standing ovation from the fans. You only get one major league debut, and Art made sure that mine was magical.

I distinctly remember sitting at my locker right after the game ended, deep in thought. Instead of celebrating my first win in the big leagues, I was hearing Dad's voice echoing inside my head, "Three hundred wins in the major leagues, Barry."

This was a goal we set early on in my life. Winning three hundred in the major leagues is the pinnacle in baseball. Twenty victories in a single season is a lifetime achievement by itself, but then do that for fifteen seasons. Get the picture? Winning three hundred in "the show" all but guarantees you to be a first-ballot Hall of Famer and forever earns you the title of "legend" in the game. So after hearing Dad's voice remind me of our lofty goal, I let out a big sigh and whispered out loud, "One down—299 to go."

The Next Level

After my first few games, seeing myself on ESPN replays was very surreal. While out at a bar or restaurant, I often suddenly fixated on the TV screen, pinching myself at the sight of Peter Gammons or some other famous analyst talking about me. But it got even better. ESPN actually contacted me and wanted to send Ann Werner, one of the first female sportscasters for the network, out on the road to interview me in my hotel room.

They were intrigued by the stories written about me in the Bay Area of how I traveled with a couple of stuffed animals that Sophie had given me and brought my own Tempur-Pedic pillow covered in a pink satin pillowcase that my mom had sewn for me. My only goal was that I just wanted to feel more at home out on the road. But evidently those details were newsworthy.

So on the day that Ann came to my hotel room in Cleveland with a camera crew, I went all out. I bought twenty more stuffed animals and dozens of candles and incense to really play up the eccentric vibe for my national TV debut. If they wanted a story, I was going to make sure they had a good one.

The interview went great and Ann kept laughing at how strange it was for a pro ballplayer to travel with such peculiar things. The fact that some TV attention and a little fame could so easily pull me away from who I truly was proved to be a sign of things to come.

Being raised in the Bronx, my dad was a big baseball fan. He always talked about Yankee Stadium and all the legendary players he watched there. So with New York on our schedule, I was not only going to play in the iconic stadium but also go up against Roger Clemens, five-time Cy Young Award winner. That dude dominated my baseball card collection growing up.

In Yankee tradition, the fans in the right field bleachers always chanted the names of each guy on the field as the team warmed up just before the first inning. They continued until the player turned to acknowledge the fans, and then the next player's chant began. Each of the nine players on the field had their own moment and then returned the love back to the bleachers. Even the starting pitcher, who was hyperfocused throwing his eight warm-up pitches, stopped to give a few seconds to follow the tradition.

Watching the player-fan connection in that park was so surreal.

In New York, baseball is religion. It doesn't get any more "big league" than being on the same field where Babe Ruth played. And the crazy thing was, you could actually *feel* the history.

In the game, matching up against Clemens was such a defining moment for me. The two-time defending World Champions' lineup featured superstars Derek Jeter, Bernie Williams, and Dave Justice. I pitched almost seven innings, allowing just one earned run, and came out with a 3–2 lead. In the ninth inning, we sent our stud closer Jason Isringhausen out to the mound to seal the deal. Two pitches later, the game was over. Bernie Williams and Dave Justice hit back-to-back home runs off Izzy and we lost the game 4–3. Regardless, I had performed well and got to pitch against one of my heroes.

People often say, and I fully agree, that there is playing in the major leagues and then there is playing in Yankee Stadium. I don't think players feel the same about the new stadium, but that old one had a mystical energy like no other park on the planet. You could somehow sense the presence of Mantle, Maris, Ruth, and Gehrig as you stood in the outfield grass.

If the big leagues was "Four-A Ball," then playing the Yankees in Yankee Stadium was "Five-A." I was already performing strong around the country, but taking on the Yanks at home with their ace on the mound was definitely another level. I had come to the Big Apple and made a statement on the field that I could play and win against *anyone*.

Following that game, one of the veterans on the team called my hotel room and said, "Be in the lobby in fifteen minutes." As a rookie, I didn't question; I just obeyed. He took me to a bar, and I didn't end up leaving until six in the morning, riding the high of playing great at Yankee Stadium. That night I didn't meet just another girl at a bar, but I ended up with the woman who owned the place. She closed and locked the entry door at 2:00 a.m. and we stayed until the sun came up. My goal was to dominate on and off the field, out to show the world I could conquer life.

Starting major league pitchers have more opportunities to make bad decisions than any other player on the team because you only work once every *fifth* day. Sure, we had to work out, run, lift, and throw bullpens, all the normal regimens to stay in shape, but we had far more downtime in our travels than our teammates. We were taught that the sleep you got two nights before your game was the most crucial. And I had always committed to a good night's rest the night before a game. But that still left three nights to do pretty much whatever we wanted. Often, we stayed out all night. If a player was "the man" in the club by night, he was more likely to take the field with a testosterone-fueled competitive edge by day. But as long as the performance on the field was good, no one cared.

For example, if I pitched a Thursday afternoon game in Detroit, then flew to Chicago for a three-game series, my next start wasn't until Tuesday. I had three nights free in the Windy City. Like everyone else, I was at the field working hard for eight to ten hours a day, but I wasn't on the lineup card. Being that we played mostly night games, I could just sleep until noon and still get my eight hours in before I had to catch the team bus to the yard. Even if I was still hung over and a little tired, I was fine. But a position player can't party all night, because he has to be fully focused *for every game in every city.*

Big league teams can feel a lot like a fraternity, especially on road trips when all the guys are riding one bus and staying in the same hotel. But it's a five-star fraternity, complete with luxury suites, four-figure dinner tabs, and the fame to secure the best table at the hottest nightclubs. Those road trips became my constant power play as I slowly started losing touch with the real world. I was living in a fantasy where people were chanting my name on the field, and girls were fighting for my attention off the field.

One of my teammates and I had a saying: "We got 'em all fooled." While people often seemed to view us like cartoon superheroes, we knew the truth about ourselves: we were just normal dudes with abnormal talent. And major issues. While we were being treated like cultural idols, we knew in our hearts we were just big kids playing out our childhood fantasies, on and off the field, riding high on the pedestal that pro sports provided.

The bottom line is that I started buying into the lies about who I was. Even though I didn't come off as arrogant or treat people badly, under the surface, a new identity was creeping in that was fictional at best, and full-blown delusional at its worst.

The Fight in the Fame

As a twenty-two-year-old ballplayer, once I began walking into bars and restaurants, getting treated as if I was the most important person in the room, I started believing it was true. When out in public, there were times I thought I was above "regular people" and gracing others with my presence.

Throughout my childhood, my father and mother always told me how special I was compared to others, that I was a champion, and how I was destined to become an even greater one. I have a birthmark on my left wrist that led to a prophecy from my mom. Just after I was born, she said, "He is going to do something special with that hand." Now there were thousands upon thousands of people echoing that same message with their words and actions alike. *But humans just cannot handle being worshipped.*

I was struggling more and more to act humble. I recall one time driving out of the A's parking lot after a game while a group of fans was waiting for an autograph. They recognized me through my tinted windows and started yelling my name. I stopped the car and rolled down the window, saying, "Hey, listen, I'm just like you guys. I'm one of you. I just throw a ball for a living."

They responded with cheers and said, "That's why we love you, Zito!"

Even after those moments, I questioned myself as to whether I only said those things to win their approval, wondering if even my humility was a lie. There was a constant tug-of-war going on inside me between the truth and the lies. On one side was the innocent kid in me that was truly amazed that people knew my name and thought I was interesting. On the other was this self-centered monster growing inside, fueled by attention and devouring the fame every chance I got. My identity was getting very muddy.

The earlier pattern of partying on the road while keeping my nose clean at home also started to blur. A group of us players made friends with a guy in Oakland who owned a string of bars and restaurants. He was constantly throwing parties and inviting us. During this time, even though I hadn't smoked pot since high school, I started up again because it made me feel even more like a rock star. To make matters worse, I was still dating Sophie, and when all the guys had their wives or girlfriends with them, I was solo, which made those nights really difficult for me. She was always superbusy, focused on getting her degree and playing Division 1 sports.

In the final game of the 2000 season, we clinched the American League West and earned home field advantage in the playoffs. We were scheduled to face the Yankees again, but this time in the pressure-filled postseason. We split the first two games in Oakland and then lost game three in New York. So now down two games to one in a five-game series, I was scheduled to pitch an elimination game in Yankee Stadium. If we lost, our season was over, but if we won, we could get the series back home to Oakland for the all-important game five.

As I was warming up in the bullpen for my big game, the New

York fans were leaning over the rail yelling every kind of obscenity about my mother they could think of to try and rattle me. But I was locked in. Taking the mound in Yankee Stadium in the playoffs was yet another box to check on my career to-do list.

Back in the dugout before the game began, I was sitting there taking in the explosive energy of October baseball in New York. My pitching coach, Rick Peterson, was at the end of the dugout. He had been watching me as I was looking around at the packed-out stadium with a sense of awe. He smiled at me and in that calming tone of his said, "Pretty cool, huh, bud?"

The most challenging thing I found about pro ball was, sadly, that those wide-eyed, awe-filled moments eventually fade away. Unpredictably, the game becomes a job. Work. Normal. You slowly stop looking up at the stands at all and no longer feel the energy from the fans like before. But one of the great qualities I loved about Rick was how he worked hard to remind me to stop, look up, and soak it in. What I didn't realize at the time was that, over the years, those truths he reminded me of would slip further and further away.

In the first inning, our cleanup hitter Olmedo Saenz hit a three-run homer off Roger Clemens. When we got our three outs and the team was taking the field, Rick looked at me and asked, "How ya doin', bud?"

I cracked a smile and answered, "This is gonna be fun, Pete."

As I took the mound, I wanted to bask in the moment and stare up at the same towering bleachers that so many legends before me had. Pitching in the exact spot where Don Larsen threw his immortalized perfect game in the World Series was both invigorating and intimidating. But feeding off the historic energy of that place, I felt like a rock star out there and attacked hitters with fervor. I ended up throwing five and two-thirds innings and gave up one run. We crushed them 11–1.

Even though we went back to Oakland for game five, we lost

and were knocked out of the playoffs. But for me, I felt the season ended on a high note. The next day after I pitched, in Roger Clemens's press interview, he said, "I was in the clubhouse changing my undershirt for the next inning and realized I got to get back out there because that kid was making short work of our lineup." That "kid" was me! And that was another amazing moment. I couldn't believe Roger made a comment about my pitching.

After that season I not only had my first big league baseball card but mine was also featured on the cover of the Bowman Box. Card companies were coming after me, paying me for my autograph. Reps often came to my Hollywood apartment with thousands of cards for me to sign at two to three bucks a pop.

Reconnecting with Regular Life

Starting the off-season in 2000 back home in LA, I called Sophie and told her, "All of my major league dreams are coming true, and with so much in front of me, I think it's best if I go at this on my own."

She began to cry and didn't understand why we should break up. "You just got home. Why are you doing this now? Let's just be together since we are both in LA. We can have this talk later, like when you go back to baseball next season."

But I was struggling inside. I knew my heart was no longer in the relationship because of what was happening on the road. Although I had already broken her trust, I wanted to be as respectful as I could of her heart. I knew cutting ties was the best thing to do but hated that I was hurting someone I cared about, so I agreed to try a little longer.

As much as I felt like a rock-god during the season, I was a tiny fish in a big pond once I got home. Hollywood doesn't care about sports stars, and certainly not for teams outside of LA. Any C-list actor could cut the line to get into a club before me. To do right by Sophie, I stayed true to her and we spent as much time as we could together.

In the off-season, I never deviated from my disciplined workout routines. I always took four weeks off without touching a ball to rest and reset for the next eleven months of work ahead. Then I started back on November 1 by getting up at 6:00 a.m. to drive forty-five minutes out to the hills of Calabasas. No later than 7:30 a.m., I was working out at the National Academy of Sports Medicine. I trained with Dr. Michael Clark, who wrote the NASM certification that most fitness trainers use today. There were always Olympic athletes in his facility, as well as NFL and NBA players too.

After my morning workout, I went back home to play guitar or hang out with Sally. That year, she and I had moved a couple of miles north to an apartment on Formosa Avenue, smack-dab in the middle of Sunset and Hollywood Boulevards. The landlord was a Russian man who barely spoke English. Our complex had everything from drug dealers to gypsies to sweet old ladies, all classic Hollywood characters. I'm pretty sure one of the women borrowed our vacuum and then sold it back to us in a street sale a few months later.

I also hired a private guitar teacher who began to show me musical modes and key scales. I didn't want to just be a campfire performer. I wanted to know exactly how music worked so I could write songs on my own one day. What I quickly realized was that music theory connected the side of my brain that loved math and science to the musicianship I'd been gifted through Mom and Dad's DNA.

Great Expectations

When February finally came, I packed up the trusty Durango and took the six-hour pilgrimage east to another spring training in

Scottsdale, Arizona. I said goodbye to Sophie in front of my place and hit the road. I arrived at my apartment in Tempe, rooming with an older player who was a friend. After just a few days there, guys started inviting me to go out on the town in the baseball-player friendly Scottsdale nightclub scene. I couldn't continue an exclusive relationship in good conscience, so I called Sophie and broke up with her on the phone. I remember her saying at the end of the conversation, "So, this is it, huh?" We said goodbye for the very last time.

Tim Hudson, Mark Mulder, and I had become a trio of pitchers known as "the Big Three." I was slotted to be the third starter. There was a lot of hype about us as a unit, and the attention on me was growing. I changed my number to 75 that spring because 34 was already retired by the great Rollie Fingers. I intentionally chose a very high number to keep it my entire career, no matter what team I played for. I thought ZITO looked great sitting symmetrically on top of the 75, creating a "shelf" that fit perfectly with my four-letter name.

After three games, my ERA was over six. *Humiliating.* For the first time in my life I stopped pitching to *win* and started pitching to *not lose.* I became afraid of failing and began doing everything I could to maintain all the momentum I had built up since getting to the big leagues. Key word being *maintain.* I was self-sabotaging my career. For four months my games were an up-and-down mental roller coaster, mostly down. I even squandered the opportunity to pitch against my hometown San Diego Padres in the stadium I grew up attending. I put too much pressure on myself to dominate and ended up losing.

Three months into the season, while sitting in the A's locker room, the scouting director that was responsible for signing me out of college confronted me and said, "Z, where'd the magic go, man?" I felt terrible and knew I was failing everyone around me.

In the midst of these struggles my father began riding my agent to hire a marketing team that could help create an image for me outside of baseball. Dad always told me I was handsome and could transcend baseball fame. He also said if I handled my work on the field, he could take care of the rest. Although the idea of being famous was alluring, my gut was telling me to stay focused on my pitching and not get caught up in that. But I kept my mouth shut and let Dad manage my career like he always had.

I became more desperate that summer to succeed, and by the end of July my self-worth was riding on each game's outcome. Before that 2001 season, when I had a bad game or two, my core confidence was unaffected. But my self-belief all those years was never mine at all. The foundation of how I thought about myself had always been shaped by what my father believed about me. Nobody else's opinion mattered, sometimes not even my own. Regardless of a setback, if Dad said I was still a great pitcher, then I believed him. But suddenly thousands of other opinions were affecting me, and now he wasn't there to protect my mind-set and keep me insulated by the bubble of self-esteem he had created. My father was no longer in my ear every day saying, "Barry, you're a great champion. You're so much greater than what these people think of you."

On July 19, 2001, we played the Twins in Minnesota. I gave up five runs, allowing eleven guys to reach base. Five days later, I was back in Oakland facing the Twins again. This time I went two innings, allowing six runs. Devastated, I started worrying about getting sent down to Triple-A and was terrified to get back on a mound again in five days.

My parents had driven up to watch that home game. They always stayed over at my town house to drive back home the next day. If the game went well, we enjoyed our time together and just had small talk. But if it went poorly, like an intense therapy session, my parents psychoanalyzed my pitching mind-set to try and figure out what went wrong.

Following that bad game, Dad said, "Barry, I'd like to stay up here with you for a few days. Mom can go back home in the morning. I have some ideas of how we can get your mind back where it needs to be, so you can be the great champion that you are." As usual, I didn't question Dad's plan. I just went with it. Plus I was willing to try *anything* to fix my pitching.

Giants and Grasshoppers

The next morning, after Mom left to drive back to LA, Dad said the same thing he'd told me all my life: "Barry, let's get to work." This was the first time since I had started playing pro ball that Dad had stepped back in as a coach and mentor. He pulled out a book from the year 1919 called *Creative Mind* by Ernest Holmes. The first few pages sounded much like the first chapter of the book of John in the Gospels, going into the origins of the universe and how something was created from nothingness. But rather than the God of the Bible, Holmes talked about "the universal mind" that permeates all of life. According to his book, there is one mind that is the "source" of everything, and we are all a part of it. Therefore, through our own individual points of consciousness, we are always accessing the one "universal mind."

Dad explained how he had made these exact discoveries early in his own life long before reading them in this book. The content was so thought-provoking that we'd have to put the book down every few sentences to unpack the ideas. While working diligently, we were only getting through a page or two per hour.

The main message of this teaching was that I could never outperform my own concept of myself. I couldn't be scared of pitching poorly and then somehow just show up and dominate the field. I had to get my expectations back up. Dad asked, "Barry, do you think when Tim Hudson goes out to the mound, he thinks, 'There's no way I can get any of these guys out'? No. Tim has a belief in himself that he is greater than his opponent. What about Pedro Martinez? He also has an incredible belief about himself, and that belief is the invisible cause for his visible pitching domination. You see, Barry, nobody can see the cause, they only see the outer effect in the world. But you can't have one without the other."

Shaken by my inability to "cause" the success that I wanted more than anything, I began to wonder, *How can I feel confident if I haven't pitched well in months?* I was forced to manufacture absolute conviction in my pitching skills from scratch. On this quest to create confidence where none existed, we made affirmation tapes. My father gave me his microcassette tape player and I started recording myself saying phrases like, "I am the best pitcher in baseball," "My fastball is 95 mph," and "I strike out hitters with ease."

At night, I often fell asleep to my own voice telling me how great I was at pitching. The goal was for the affirmations to sink into my subconscious and eventually become my own thoughts and feelings. I could then project those out into the "one universal mind" that would, according to "universal law," manifest everything I was affirming back into my reality. Literally, mind over matter. Dick Mills's anchor statements on posters that I had used in college were one thing, but this was next-level metaphysical stuff for me.

Over the next several days, even when we left to run errands, Dad and I still worked through the pages of *Creative Mind*. In some ways, I felt like a kid again with his coaching me in my mind-set. Because I trusted my father, I bought in fully to this new way of thinking.

After a couple of days working through the book, the time came for my between-start bullpen session with Rick. I returned home from the field ecstatic, telling Dad, "Rick suggested I open up my stride today, and when I did, my fastball really started poppin' and my command was better than it's been all year!"

Dad quietly put his hand on my shoulder and said, "Barry, you see what is happening? It's already starting to work. The universe is responding to your thoughts." He glanced over at the book on the table, then back at me, and nodded as I processed his words.

I responded, "Oh my gosh! You are so right, Dad. There's no way this is a coincidence."

Once Dad pointed out the connection, I was convinced in that moment that my "mental work," as we called it, had actually created my breakthrough on the mound that day. What we believed, based on the book, was that since we are all part of the one "universal mind," then Rick Peterson was a part as well, and what I had believed and was speaking into the universe was causing Rick to tell me to tweak my pitching delivery. After that experience, I had total conviction in "the creative mind" way of life. I felt that I alone was in charge of my own fate. So my father and I kept studying.

In one of those sessions, Dad told me, "He who sees himself as a grasshopper is a grasshopper, but he who sees himself as a giant is a giant." I was convinced that while I had been a grasshopper when I pitched against Minnesota, I was indeed becoming a giant who could tower over my next opponent.

Augmented Reality

My next start was on July 29, a Sunday day game at home against the Kansas City Royals. I walked into the clubhouse feeling like I was keeping a secret that no one else knew but were all about to find out—I was the best pitcher in baseball. I saw sportswriter Jeff Pearlman and told him, "Watch what I do the rest of the season." Struggling as I had been that year, I had never before made such a "dig me" comment to anyone, but I now had total conviction.

In the game, I dominated the Royals, not allowing a runner past second base while striking out nine. I viewed myself as a giant, and the opposing team as grasshoppers, just as Dad had told me. I had made a 180-degree turn in just five days.

What I came to realize years later was that had it just been me and that *Creative Mind* book, I would have been saying, "There's no way I am the best pitcher in baseball. Just look at my stats." But because my dad was making these declarations in connection with the book, I believed them wholeheartedly.

The Royals game sparked the best streak of my career. I won ten of my next twelve starts while averaging just over one run allowed per nine innings. I shut out the red-hot Boston Red Sox as well as the Cleveland Indians, who were the best hitting team in baseball. One hundred percent all in on my new mind-set, I went from being statistically one of the worst pitchers in the league those first four months to being the league's top pitcher in August and September, receiving American League Pitcher of the Month awards for both months.

My self-belief snowballed with each dominating game. I initially believed my mind was a part of God's universal mind, but after being so successful those months, I eventually felt like I *was God*. I was convinced I was creating reality as He creates reality, because as I was speaking things out into the universe, they were manifesting perfectly in my life. While these confessions sound a little crazy, I know they were merely symptoms of my desperate search for truth.

Winning 102 games in 2001, my team went to the playoffs and faced the Yankees for the second year in a row. We won the first two games in New York, and I was slated to pitch game three back in Oakland and potentially knock the Yankees out of the playoffs.

But two nights before my start, something odd occurred. I had a powerful negative thought pattern enter my mind. Since I was the league's hottest pitcher, I knew everyone was *expecting* me to dominate the Yankees. I became very unsettled and felt anxiety rise up for the first time in my life. I woke up that next morning in a sheer panic, thinking, "What if I go out there and fail miserably?"

Fear started to overwhelm me. A random thought flashed through my mind: "Maybe I'm not as in charge of my fate as I thought I was?" I knew I believed there was one universal mind and that I was in control of it, yet I began questioning whether some *other force* could be toying with me, making me believe I was invincible, but then overnight have me scared to death.

Finally, just before my big game, I was able to reel myself back in and get my head straight. I dominated again, giving up just two hits and one run, but we lost 1–0. Then we dropped the next two games, which knocked us out of the running for the 2001 World Series. Even with my momentary bout with anxiety, I closed out that season believing I had figured out the secret to life. I now felt I could manifest *any* reality I desired. And thought that if my mindset was powerful enough, I could even influence the outcome of others' actions.

I could believe *anything* into existence that I willed.

Dangerous, deadly thoughts for a twenty-three-year-old in the spotlight.

Barry's Basics—Third Base

Because the next major step in my career was my first contract negotiation, I want to take a moment to explain that process. Upon getting called up to the big leagues, a player will be paid the major league minimum salary, which is a predetermined amount each year. Most guys will play their first three seasons in the big leagues earning the minimum. But once a player has three full seasons in the league, he can either agree with the team on a contract for the next year, or if no agreement can be reached, he can go through the grueling arbitration process to get paid what he feels he is worth. He can do this for three years until becoming a free agent. If a player is good enough to eventually get through six full seasons, he becomes an unrestricted free agent where he can hit the open market and decide to play for the highest bidder. That's when and where the big money comes in.

The arbitration process is exactly how it sounds in that the player and his agent haggle with his team over his value in front of a panel. In short, the team works to prove you're worthless while you work to prove you're priceless. Just like when selling a house, selling a player has everything to do with the comps for showing value.

The agent creates a list of highly paid current MLB players who have similar stats and service time as his client and attempts to persuade the panel why the team should pay the player more than the team is offering. Meanwhile, the team has already submitted the salary number they are willing to pay, and they attempt to explain why the player is worth no more than their offer. After all arguments from both sides have been presented, the panel selects either the player *or* the club's proposed dollar amount as the salary for the upcoming season. No negotiations. One of the sums wins.

But another way that players and teams can agree on a contract is on a long-term deal, which can happen anytime before the three-year arbitration date. However, this option is available only to the highest-level performers in the game. In this case, the team sees value in "locking up" a young player because they project that he will perform well over many years. Rather than pay the player a lot of money in arbitration each year, they'd rather give him a lump sum up front to ensure that he will *not* go into arbitration. Over the life of the contract, this option saves the team money as long as the player maintains performance and doesn't get hurt. Although the player risks leaving some future arbitration money on the table, the long-term deal would serve the player immensely in the event that he got injured or did not perform well, because the salary is guaranteed. While this process can be risky for both sides, rarely will a young player turn down millions of dollars that get flashed in his face.

Creating My Own Monster

"I'm here at the highest levels of baseball and I'm working every day to be one of the best. It's just a constant journey within myself to see how much of me I can bring out."

—My interview in *Science of Mind* magazine[1]

Well, Barry, Huddy was second in Cy Young voting in 2000 and Mulder was second last year. Now in the 2002 season, is it your turn to be second?" asked Susan Slusser, a writer for the *San Francisco Chronicle*.

"Yeah, I guess so," I answered with a patronizing laugh.

But I thought to myself, *No way I'm coming in second. I'm going to win this year.*

Knowing the high expectations from the team, fans, and media heading into the 2002 spring training, Susan had requested an interview with the Big Three—Hudson, Mulder, and me. After a great season in 2001, breaking the 100-win barrier, a huge milestone for any team, we were getting accustomed to all the attention.

Holding firm to my and Dad's agreed-upon mind-set, being first was the reality I had chosen. But that was my secret to keep because I didn't want to come across as arrogant. For months I had already been "planting seeds," as Dad often said, that the Cy Young would be mine in 2002.

After the *San Francisco Chronicle* interview, while stretching during warm-ups before a game, Huddy looked at me and said, "Hey Z, as long as Pedro Martinez is in our league, we ain't gettin' no Cy Young, bro." I smiled and nodded but then thought, *Huddy's creating his own reality. My reality is, Pedro or no Pedro, I'm winning the Cy Young this year.* Further evidence of how immersed I was in the "creative mind" way of thinking. As the regular season began, I picked up right where I left off the previous year, winning four of my first five starts.

But all too soon, the proof that my life philosophy was built on a shaky foundation flew in my face while I was pitching in Yankee Stadium. In the first inning, a weak ground ball from Jorge Posada went right through my legs as the Yanks scored their first run. I went on to give up five more runs before getting pulled. After the game, feeling totally defeated, I was very angry and scolded myself internally. *Z, don't ever let them humiliate you like that again. Be a man!* My encroaching ego had been threatened for the first time since the "creative mind" turnaround.

At the next game in Chicago, I took the field with my forced bravado at the helm, thinking, *Take no prisoners and be a man, Barry!* I began pitching solely to stave off the negative opinions from others. I even wrote reminders under the bill of my hat, like "Kill or be killed." In the next game, I beat the White Sox, went on to win nine of my next ten decisions, and earned my first all-star game selection. I was doing everything I could on and off the field to prove my manhood. With these new macho demands on myself from within, the monster inside was growing.

The Making of "The Man"

In May, my agent began negotiations with the team while I stayed focused on pitching. I took an 11–3 record into the all-star break, which is right around the time I signed my four-year deal for $18 million. That agreement took me up to free agency, so now I didn't have to worry about the arbitration process and could just keep pitching. That summer, our team won twenty straight games to tie the American League record and we got into the playoffs for a third straight year, this time against the Minnesota Twins. While I won my game, we lost the series. I ended up with a league-leading 23 wins and a 2.75 ERA in 2002. Those stats made *everybody* happy.

On the morning of November 7, 2002, I was in San Francisco when my agent called. He broke the news that I had been awarded the Cy Young and needed to be at a press conference in Oakland that afternoon at 1:00 p.m.

At twenty-four years old, I was the fourth-youngest player to ever win the award and the youngest since 1986 when Roger Clemens received his first. Pedro Martinez had won in 1999 and 2000. I had received seventeen first-place votes to Pedro's eleven, making him second. Although Pedro had a lower ERA, I had more wins and had played a major role in the team's momentum. My record was 13–1 after a team loss, which the sportswriters felt was enough to vote me in for the award.[2]

The way my dad and I saw things, the Cy Young was a great honor but also a strong confirmation that everything I was *on the inside* was now being seen as an effect in the visible world. Life inside out. The universal mind was giving back everything I was thinking into it, namely, "Barry Zito is the man!" Dad felt like he had fully integrated his long-standing worldview into my life and now I was breathing rare air in baseball, just like we'd planned for years.

Together, *we* created my reality of baseball success. And honestly, because of Dad's lofty standards and goals for my career, getting the Cy Young was just the beginning. He often told me, "Barry, you have earned *one* so far, but you can win *ten* of these, so don't ever stop planting your seeds."

During the 2002 season, my father hired my own PR person, telling me "every big star needs a publicist." Not knowing why I needed one, I still agreed because Dad always knew better. He said he wanted to "boost my visibility" to the world so I could become a "household name." I learned that almost no other baseball players had a personal publicist and just used the team's PR department to field requests. But having my own rep like the Hollywood stars made me feel special compared to my teammates. On top of that, I had a better chance to be on magazine covers and TV shows now that my publicist was paid to get those gigs for me. After winning, the media attention heated up like crazy, and the publicist could help capitalize.

A major sportswriter for *ESPN the Magazine* had requested a sit-down interview and I had invited him to come to the little Hollywood apartment where Sally and I lived. The reporter said when he pulled up out front, he thought, *There is no way Barry Zito lives in these crappy apartments.* Because I had given him the address but not our unit number, he got out of his car, stood out front, and started yelling, "Barry! Hey, Barry!" Knowing he was coming, I laughed, walked out to greet him, and invited him up. I suppose because of the way I had been raised, even though I had money now, I was happy living a simple life with my sister in the middle of the Hollywood circus.

Ironically, the awards that came my way were never really my actual goals. My father always taught me to strive for "pitching excellence" and then *everything else* would follow. My coach Rick Peterson often reminded me of a similar truth, saying, "Even though the icing gets bigger and sweeter, always keep your focus on the cake, Z." With all the attention my pitching was creating, something was shifting in me. I slowly started to believe that I was really as interesting as the sportswriters said I was. I was set apart in the baseball world as an "eccentric surfer yoga dude." I liked that I had a budding identity off the field that gave me approval, and I subtly began to crave more and more to feed the monster.

Just as the ESPN sportswriter was surprised that I lived in my run-down apartment, so was one of my neighbors. "Drug Dealer Dave," as we called him, approached me one day. "Dude! Barry, seriously, why do you still live in this nasty complex? You are a major league stud and you just won the Cy Young! What are you thinking?"

Appreciative of his concern, I responded, "Well, I'm really comfortable here, Dave."

Confused by my answer, yet determined to make his point, he added, "Seriously, Zito, you should be living large up in the Hills."

Now I was the one who was puzzled. "The *Hills*? What are you talking about?"

The street dealer continued his real estate advice. "The Hollywood Hills. Right up there," he answered as he looked into the distance and pointed to the north. While I had lived in LA awhile, I was barely in the Hollywood scene and certainly had no idea where the famed Hills neighborhoods were.

Before my 2002 season, I had bought a nice flat in San Francisco's Marina district to live during the season. I was the only A's player who lived in the city and drove across the Bay Bridge every day. Even though the place was only twelve hundred square feet, because of its premium location by the water, the price tag was over $700,000. Another reason I had bought a home in the Bay Area was because, at that point, I was a much bigger fish there than in LA. But I was hoping to change that soon enough.

A buddy of mine in the Hollywood scene called me one night and said, "We're going to Jeff Green's house tonight, so get ready for a crazy time." We drove to the top of Sunset Plaza Drive, ironically only a few miles from my apartment, but light-years away from anything I had ever experienced. As we turned north off Sunset and ascended up the hill, I asked, "Dude, is *this* the Hollywood Hills?" He laughed, as if it was crazy for an LA resident to ask such a question.

After going through security at the front gate, we walked into the three-story mansion to see famous actors and fashion models everywhere. We made our way through the party and out to the balcony where I looked over the shimmering skyline of Los Angeles. I thought back to Drug Dealer Dave's advice. He was so right! What was I doing in my crappy apartment when I could live the high life up here?

Within the week, I had my Bay Area real estate agent list my flat in San Francisco. We sold the place in no time, so I told my real estate agent in LA that I wanted a house in the Hills. She set up three showings, with the third house being only a few away from Jeff Green's mansion, where I initially fell in love with the neighborhood. I was certain it was fate.

The house had belonged to legendary actor Burt Reynolds, with wall-to-wall fifteen-foot windows and sprawling views down to Orange County. From the bedroom on one side of the house, I could see downtown, and then from the back balcony on the other side, the ocean. I was hooked and couldn't believe what I had been missing. And all because of the sage advice of a street-level drug dealer who cared enough about me to tell me of this new land I knew not of. Before I left, I gifted Dave with a game-used jersey as a token of my appreciation.

Soon, Sally and I pulled away from our Formosa Avenue apartment one last time and moved into my new mansion. The closest house below ours belonged to Britney Spears. I used to joke that I could throw a baseball into her pool. And I actually could have.

Although my backyard past the pool and deck was nothing but a very steep hill, Dad encouraged me to construct a bullpen back there, or better said, *down* there. So I hired a crew to terrace out a perfectly flat runway on the hill for a regulation pitcher's mound. When I made an errant throw, that baseball was lost forever, somewhere down the canyon.

No matter what was happening in my personal life, I was always dedicated to a strict routine of working out and honing my pitching skills. But my commitment to structure bled over into my personal life and relationships. The pattern with girlfriends became as predictable as my workout regimen. I always had a steady dating relationship through the off-season because I had the time and I could stay in one place for a few months. But once baseball started back, the game always took priority. In fact, that's exactly what I told the girls every time during my breakup conversations: "I'm married to baseball."

Dad had always instilled in me that baseball required full focus during the season. When he knew I was steadily dating someone, he often checked up on me to see if a relationship was getting too serious and therefore becoming a distraction. During the season I was still meeting girls on the road and at home, but my heart was rarely involved.

Keeping Score

There are two types of accolades that a player can receive in baseball: personal and team awards. I had always heard players talk about how a World Series was the greatest honor, but I was so high on my new Cy Young that I wasn't at all sure that was true. Only three seasons in, I figured there was plenty of time left in my career for the team honors. I knew if my personal pitching performances were as strong as possible, my team, of course, benefitted too. So I continued pursuing the lofty self-focused goals Dad had planted in me of three hundred wins, the pinnacle for any major league pitcher.

But as the 2003 season began, the concept of maintaining and protecting my stellar pitching reputation was setting in. One day as I was standing in the outfield shagging balls and contemplating my season, I began to do some math that brought on a dangerous threat to my ego. Six weeks into another great season, I was 6–3 with a 2.50 ERA, but at 23–5 the previous year, that meant I had to win 17 of my final 26 starts. As if that wasn't difficult enough, I could only lose two of those starts to stay on pace with my Cy Young stats from 2002. But to maintain the attention and momentum on *and* off the field, those were the numbers I had to achieve. With that realization, fear overcame me. Doubts arose. Questions rushed in. Suddenly, my mind didn't feel quite so "creative." I had realized an almost impossible equation and expectation.

The absolute crazy fact was, up to that moment, my overall record for my first three seasons was 47–17. I was already well on my way to three hundred wins. Twenty seasons in that range and I could attain pitching immortality. The numbers I posted through my first three years were the best start of *any* pitching career in the history of baseball, even beating out my heroes Sandy Koufax and Roger Clemens. But the question crept into my heart, *How am I going to keep up this historic pace?* I may have set the bar very high for myself, but now so did the baseball world. Because I was taking full credit for my success, I began to feel the weight of all the newly created expectations too.

After bad games, I started projecting my own negative opinions of myself on others around me, even random strangers. If a guy at the neighborhood coffee shop was looking my direction, but wasn't appearing overly excited at seeing his local sports hero, I was sure he was thinking to himself what a terrible pitcher I was. Fascinating how when you think too highly of yourself you can swear everyone believes you are amazing when you do well. But at the same time, you're certain they despise you when you underperform. The bottom line was that, good or bad, it was all about *me*.

That was the first season that shame began to creep into my heart. I regularly assumed if I had a few tough games that everyone was judging me. I actually started hiding out at my house when I didn't do well, but then went out and about in the city, head held high, when I played great. I was projecting the idea of my father onto everyone around me—loving me when I did well, let down when I failed. All love or all shame, no middle ground. My self-worth started being shaped by the outcome of games and the opinions of others. I had strapped myself tightly into the seat of an emotional roller coaster and had no idea how to make the ride stop.

That year I started getting into photography and bought a Canon 1D. Living in a rental flat in the Marina during the season, I often frequented a high-end camera shop a block away on Chestnut Street. One morning following a bad game the night before against the Angels, I walked into the shop especially paranoid. The guy behind the counter who had helped me in the past innocently said, "Oh, hey Barry. Man, tough game last night, huh? You were struggling out there."

Feeling anger boil up inside, I shot him as violent a look as I could. Since I trusted this guy, I entered the shop with my guard down but now felt threatened and ashamed. I backpedaled out the door without a word. With a bruised ego, I walked back to my flat feeling sad that I could no longer hang in my favorite camera shop anymore. The walls my fear was building were getting higher and beginning to close in around me.

The clerk was only attempting to be compassionate and personal with me like a friend. But all I heard was rejection and judgment. The camera store situation was a prime example of how easily my ego could be shattered by *anyone*.

That summer we stayed at the Ritz-Carlton in Philadelphia for a three-game set with the Phillies. One evening after a game, a fan quietly approached me in the hotel bar. "Mr. Zito," she said, "you must feel so blessed to have such a great curveball."

I lashed out, "Blessed?! Do you know how long I have been working on pitching in my backyard? My whole life!" She back-pedaled and apologized for bothering me. I was so offended that she had offered the notion of giving credit to anything but me for my pitching skill and success. Just further evidence that things were getting out of hand when it came to my self-worth.

BZ on TV

That summer of 2003 my publicist got me on the *Late Show with David Letterman*. By this point, I was very serious about playing guitar and writing songs. As he often did on his show, Dave wanted me to perform a stunt. He had me go over to the roof of the building across from his to throw baseballs back toward his offices to see how many windows I could shatter. But after that sequence, he wanted a short interview. Waiting for my big moment, I told everyone in the greenroom that I had a song to perform. But the producers informed me I would not be doing anything of the sort.

When I went out onstage for the interview, I decided to mention the song in my dialogue with Letterman. I said, "Yeah, Dave, I had written a song to play for you but your staff told me no. But that's okay, I can just sing it next time I'm on."

Dave, in his normal sarcastic tone, fired back, "Next time? Next time you're on?" then smirked toward the camera as if to say, "Who does this guy think he is?" I was never invited back.

In the course of those years, I was on the *Tonight Show with Jay Leno*, the *Late Late Show with Craig Ferguson*, and *Last Call with*

Carson Daly, all the LA-based late night talk shows. I also guest starred and performed on the *Chris Isaak Show* on Showtime, as well as appeared in an episode of *JAG,* the popular military legal drama, where I played . . . wait for it . . . a baseball player.

Now aside from pro ball, surfing, and songwriting, I added actor to the list. All this was feeding my ego to become a Hollywood "it person." I was building on my dad's vision for me to be a "crossover athlete," one who was known as a great player and also a celebrity name in the nonsports world. I was creating my own monster, complete with dreams of walking red carpets and being in the gossip tabloids. Dad was always behind the scenes pushing the publicist to book as many opportunities as possible. I often wonder if he was actually chasing his own aspirations for fame.

I remember a high school friend telling me as my popularity was starting to blossom, "Barry, nobody gets to live the rock star life you are, so you better go big for all of us who will never get to." Those kinds of comments from people made me feel as if it was my duty to take full advantage of the once-in-a-lifetime opportunities I had.

Unbeknownst to me, I was treading in dangerous waters with all of these aspirations for fame. In any form of entertainment in this country, people love the up-and-comer, the underdog, and the out-of-nowhere success story. But once you get to a certain level, they also love to watch you fall. We are really good at creating idols and worshipping them for a while, but when we get bored, we just take them down and replace them with a new one. That's how the phrase "fifteen minutes of fame" was created.

Exception and Entitlement

At 14–12 in 2003, my win-loss record was nothing near a Cy Young level, but my ERA and innings pitched were still tops in the league, enough to maintain my status as a big league stud. Going home to my new Los Angeles mansion with a multimillion-dollar salary, I had everything I needed to pour on the fame flame and mix into the Hollywood lifestyle. Because of my "Barry is special" upbringing and my stellar baseball performance, I felt I deserved every ounce of praise I was getting. I started to hear quite a bit of, "We normally don't do this, but for you, Mr. Zito, we will make an exception." Getting preferential treatment everywhere you go doesn't take long for most humans to begin to expect it. Entitlement sets in and you are the exception to all rules. Or so you think.

Around that same time, a "men's magazine" had requested an interview. After we were done, I asked about a girl I had seen in their pages. The staff there agreed to put us in touch, so she came to a game. Not only did we start dating but I also set up two of my old high school buddies with a couple of this girl's model friends so we could all hang out. I just saw that kind of behavior as "sharing the benefits with my boys." Predictably, that relationship didn't last long.

On the baseball front, because we constantly played the Texas Rangers, Alex Rodriguez and I became friends from seeing each other at the field so often. A common practice for pro ball players is to trade memorabilia and sign baseballs for one another. At one particular game, Alex came up to me and offered to trade a pair of his autographed game-used spikes for a signed game-used glove of mine. Happy to make the deal happen, today I still have that pair of black Nikes with the blue swoosh, signed to me from Alex. Once during the off-season, Alex came out to LA to hang out, and we went to dinner at the Asia de Cuba on Sunset, and then to the Skybar, both at the Mondrian Hotel LA. Just another night of living the high life in Hollywood, but obviously when you're seen hanging out with A-Rod, you feel especially important.

Jekyll & Hyde, Barry & BZ

In 2003, I experienced a paradigm shift where baseball became much more than the game I had played as a kid. It began to take on a bigger role in my life, giving me a strong sense of worth as a human being. Because of pro ball, I had a backstage pass to the celebrity lifestyle I had seen put on a pedestal my entire life. As a result, keeping up my Hollywood status became the ultimate destination, and baseball became the means to get me there.

But much like the classic tale of Dr. Jekyll in his battle of becoming Mr. Hyde, the more I tasted the sweetness of celebrity the more I craved, like an insatiable fame monster inside me. I wanted to be the rich and powerful playboy, no longer simply a pro baseball player. Not satisfied with just living the American dream, I was chasing a Hollywood fantasy.

When I heard guys in the locker room say, "Baseball may be what I *do*, but it's not *who* I am," I thought to myself, *This guy doesn't take the game seriously. If he were fully committed, then there should be no line between who he is and what he does.* But for me, since my stature in the game came with so many benefits, I was proud to say that I was nothing more, and nothing less, than baseball.

The irony about this time in my life is that if you were to have known me back then, you likely wouldn't have been aware of my aspirations of fame. I was still a kind and caring person, still soft-hearted and loving, but under the surface this *thing* was rising up, intoxicating me with its desires of worldly satisfaction. I would never have admitted to anyone at the time, "I just want to be famous," but unknown to even me sometimes, this was my driving motivation.

I saw zero separation in my identity as a person and my identity as a major league pitcher. I was "BZ, the rock star ballplayer" and my creed was, "Of course I am what I do because it is incredible!" The End.

But as in the story of Jekyll and Hyde, the death of the man became imminent once the transformation to the monster began.

Barry's Basics—Home Plate

After six full years of major league service time, a player becomes an unrestricted free agent. This is good for the player and bad for his current employer, especially if the guy is top-tiered. If the player can command huge numbers on the open market, his current team may offer him a long-term deal by the end of the season before he hits free agency. The team will usually expect a "hometown discount," because in most cases, they were the team that raised that player up from the minors.

Most players feel more comfortable re-upping with their current team, even if making a few million dollars less. There is a familiarity in knowing that, besides the paycheck amount, not much else is going to change in the day-to-day routine. The pressure doesn't increase near as much when a player signs a new contract with his current team in a city that already loves him, as opposed to going with a different team in a brand-new city.

The opposite scenario is when a player goes for the gold, hits the open market, and lets multiple bidders fight each other to get his signature on the dotted line. The potential downside for the player is that outside of his stature in the game, he is virtually unknown to the new home team. Losing all the credibility he had built up with his previous team and fan base, that player starts from scratch in building up respect. In the case where a player struggles out of the gate, he is on a much shorter leash with a new team than with his old team. That intense pressure is why many top-tiered players never test the open market.

8

Tattoo That Number on Your Forehead

"Barry is Joshua, and Jericho represents the state of mind he needs to attain. Only after he captures [that] can the walls be broken down."

—Joe Zito, *Sports Illustrated*[1]

Fourteen-foot indoor waterfall.

A 450-gallon saltwater aquarium.

A $150,000 sound system.

Multicolored mirrors positioned in strategic spots all over the house.

Black shag carpet so thick you couldn't see your toes.

Those were just a few of the amenities I added to my Hollywood Hills home during my complete "bachelor pad" overhaul.

But just as a python slowly and subtly wraps around its prey, my fame-induced lifestyle began to take over my life. While I knew all too well the battle raging in my heart, *something* was changing in me—but I couldn't pinpoint exactly what was going on.

Escalating Expectations

Having lived in LA for five years with my name and reputation growing, I could now get into any restaurant or club I wanted. To keep up my image during the season, I rented a penthouse apartment in Pacific Heights that overlooked the Golden Gate Bridge and Alcatraz Island. That season, an Oakland car dealership let me drive one of their brand-new Corvettes.

Whether in an exotic car, at home, or out at a club, I was striving to appear as if I were on top of my game. Being portrayed by the media as a onetime dominant pitcher who was "losing his mojo" created inner turmoil that I tried to numb out by smoking weed. During the 2004 season, if I wasn't pitching, I often smoked at the house before jumping in the 'Vette, cranking up some Pat Metheny, and heading over the Bay Bridge to the field. The THC, coupled with the calming music, helped me fend off the voices in my head that told me I would forever fall short of the expectations of being a Cy Young–caliber pitcher again.

Now five years into my major league career, baseball had completed its transformation. What was once the game I loved to play was now the only thing in my life that could deliver the approval and validation I needed to temper my insecurity. My on-field performance became more important than ever. The year 2003 represented a failed first attempt to reclaim Cy Young glory, and I feared falling short yet again of the bar I had set so high.

During the previous off-season, I had become friends with a club promoter named Josh who later became a very close friend. He made a good living by getting A-list celebrities to hang out in new clubs to create a buzz in town, which made the owners happy. He started inviting me to the hottest spots in Hollywood and seating me at tables with the stars.

At the start of the 2004 season, Josh told me about a successful actress that he thought I'd connect with. She was a season ticket holder for the Dodgers and a big baseball fan in general. Alyssa and I started out emailing, and then went on our first date in San Francisco a few weeks later. We started off casually, but quickly went into an exclusive relationship. We got along great and shared a love for music. I also felt a new type of safety with her because she understood the pressures of fame far better than I did. I truly cared for her and got along with her family, but also realized her celebrity status was boosting my own ego. The fact that she was a Hollywood A-lister created an excitement I hadn't felt before in a relationship.

By the all-star break of that season, I was 5–7 with a 4.42 ERA. While my stats weren't putting me in danger of a Triple-A demotion, they were far worse than expected. On June 21, 2004, I made my first *Sports Illustrated* cover, but not the way I had always hoped. An NBA player was the featured athlete, while I had just a small inset of my face down in the bottom right-hand corner with the caption: "Inside the Head of Barry Zito." The article began with: "As he struggles to regain his Cy Young form. . . ."[2]

When you do an interview with a major magazine, you rarely know the final spin they will place on the content you've provided. The first featured quote from me was: "I view my pitching based on how confident I was out there, period. And if I lose that confidence, I can become a prisoner in my own mind."[3] The baseball world was discovering that Barry Zito was his own worst enemy. Even though the game was becoming more and more internal for me, my laser-focus of improving my craft never wavered. At this point, I was actually working harder than ever before. Because my confidence seemed to be so unpredictable, I felt more repetitions would help me get my performance back. But no matter what I did, I was not getting the job done on the field.

By my last start of the season, our chances of postseason play were riding solely on my shoulders. If I could pitch us to victory over the Angels while another contending team lost their game that day, we could get into the playoffs. I pitched well and came out of the game after seven innings with a 4–2 lead. But our bullpen blew the game. Even though I gave us a solid chance at winning and threw 114 pitches, a heavy workload for any starter, I still got a lot of the blame for our playoff hopes being thwarted that day. One of the commentators said I had "wimped out" and should have stayed in the entire game. Ending the year that way was really tough. Given the fact that my Oakland fans had booed me throughout the season, I felt light-years away from the pitcher I had been just two years before. I finished at 11–11 with my worst ERA as a major leaguer.

The Big Three Minus Two

Coming off such a disappointing season, there was a new fire under me. I was determined that off-season to work even harder as my baseball performance and celebrity status were waning. I lifted weights, did mirror drills, and set up an old mattress to throw into like when I was a kid in my backyard.

On a large poster board in my bedroom, I created a detailed grid of all the daily and weekly baseball tasks I had to perform and checked off each one as I did it. I wanted so badly to squelch the negative chatter about my career and get back into the game's good graces. I was still dating Alyssa exclusively at the time, so my lifestyle was very focused and tame by my past standards.

In December of 2004, Alyssa and I were on vacation at a resort hotel in Yosemite. When the USA Today newspaper was delivered to the door, I instinctively went straight to the sports section. I will never forget the shock of seeing the headlines: "Mark Mulder and Tim Hudson Traded." I could not believe the Big Three had been broken up with no prior warning from the Oakland front office. I did *not* see that coming.

I knew immediately what that headline meant for me. No more sharing the load with two stud pitchers. I was now the number one guy. I sat by the fire with the snow falling outside, reading how my life had been changed. I immediately called my agent and asked him what in the world was going on. The bottom line was the A's wanted to trade Huddy and Mulder to get something in return for them before they became free agents within the next two years. They also felt that since I had never been injured, I was a good candidate to lead the team going forward, and obviously they weren't worried about my poor performance from the previous season. *But I was.*

In keeping with my relational pattern and with the impending pressure of the season, just a couple of weeks before spring training, Alyssa and I broke up. I wanted to go solo into the 2005 season, working hard to focus on my performance, and start again with, as Dad often said, "No distractions, Barry." Remember my "I'm married to baseball" mantra.

As the season began, I was incredibly uncomfortable being seen as the guy who was expected to lead the team. The last time I had been a bona fide number one starter was at USC, long before my Cy Young self-consciousness set in. I felt like I was up on the high wire now with no net to catch me. While I still kept a copy of *Creative Mind* close, my desperation for spiritual solutions to my mental state led me to routinely explore the shelves of Barnes & Noble. Searching for a new magic formula, I went deep into Buddhism, the writings of Osho, and many other Eastern religion offshoots. My search for the truth was officially in high gear. All the while still working hard to keep up the image of being "the Man" off the field, too, I began dating an Oakland Raiders cheerleader.

Sandy Koufax had presented me with my Cy Young at the MLB awards dinner in New York back in 2002, so I decided to seek him out as a resource. He graciously agreed to speak to me over the phone about pitching. Hoping he could tell me how to regain confidence in myself and offer tips on battling my crippling self-doubt, I asked Sandy how he was so successful on the mound. He answered, "Down and away, Barry, you have got to master the fastball. Down and away."

After I got off the phone, I thought to myself, *Are you kidding me? That's the key to dominating the major leagues?* Obviously Sandy never made the game as complicated as I did. I wished I could have honed my focus on only pitch selection and location like he had obviously done. As so many advised me to do over the years, keeping baseball simple was a skill I never mastered.

During batting practice before a game in Colorado, I was standing in the outfield shagging as pitchers routinely do. Only this time my back was to the hitter, a huge no-no. I was scanning the bleachers for girls when I took a screaming line drive right between the shoulder blades. Our star hitter, Nick Swisher, hit a rocket right at me and by the time I heard my teammates yelling for me to turn around, the damage was done. The strike created what they call in pro sports a full body stinger. My fingertips and toes went numb and tingled for a few minutes. That injury subluxed a few of my ribs, meaning they came out of place, which was instantly painful when I tried to breathe deeply. I battled that condition for many years after that injury, which was fortunately one of my few over the years.

While we didn't make the playoffs that season, I did manage to make improvements from 2004, ending the 2005 season at 14–13 with a 3.86 ERA. Better than 11–11, but not even close to my career high of 23–5. When you pitch thirty-five games in a season, twenty-three wins look way more impressive than fourteen.

The Big Hurt and Breakups

Starting into the 2006 season, I made the personal commitment to back off even further from the playboy lifestyle and work harder than ever to stay fully focused on the field. I had met a hostess named Cassandra at a high-end restaurant, and we started dating exclusively. Maintaining a relationship with one noncelebrity girl throughout an entire season was a step toward some relational and emotional maturity for me. Plus that commitment certainly cut down on the chaos and drama in my life. I also made the decision to rent a home in the quiet suburb community of Alamo for the season, not in San Francisco. I wanted to focus fully on baseball and eliminate off-the-field distractions for my all-important free agent season.

Seeking out great advisers as he always did, Dad invited one of the smartest men in baseball, agent Scott Boras, to sit down with me during spring training and discuss my upcoming season. Dad knew I had my biggest year in front of me, and with my résumé, if I pitched well enough, I could go into free agency as the top pitcher on the market. That could possibly bring record-setting contract numbers. I had already begun stressing about my season but Scott encouraged me to relax, just be myself on the field, and "let my talent rise to the top." I felt relieved that Scott didn't tell me I had to win another Cy Young to prove myself.

During the 2006 spring training, the Oakland A's came right out and said they couldn't afford to re-sign me. I was not surprised since they are a smaller-market team, but I knew I was really going to miss playing in Oakland. That season, young starters Danny Haren and Joe Blanton were coming into their own, filling the shoes of Mulder and Hudson. Once again having a couple of pitchers to shoulder the load could help me achieve the relaxation and self-trust that Boras had encouraged me to feel. A major highlight that year was one of my childhood heroes, Frank "the Big Hurt" Thomas, had come over to play with the A's after his many years in Chicago.

By mid-July at the all-star break, I was 8–6 with an ERA in the mid-threes. Ozzie Guillen, the White Sox skipper who was managing the American League team, had selected me for his team. Once my all-star announcement was made, Dad arranged for a special press release to go out while I was pitching my inning in the Summer Classic that stated I had signed with Scott. Because he was the top agent in baseball, we decided he was the best to represent me as a free agent.

Even getting to free agency is rare, let alone being one of the top guys on the market. Now we were sure to capitalize on the once-in-a-lifetime opportunity. So as I was on the mound facing the NL's best hitters, the all-star game commentators told a national audience, "Soon to be free agent Barry Zito will now be represented by Scott Boras." Being a "Boras guy" meant people began talking about how my contract was sure to break records.

The momentum was definitely swinging back in my favor. My cumulative major league record of 102–63 was dominating by any standard, and I had never missed a start since coming into the league seven years prior. This coupled with the fact that I had the second-most innings pitched in those seven seasons meant I had an opportunity to make history. I also didn't have a lot of competition in the free agent pitching market.

In the 2006 season, our team made the playoffs, and I was slated to pitch game one of the ALDS against Johan Santana in the Metrodome in Minnesota. Johan hadn't lost a game at home in over a year. I did my part by throwing eight innings of shutout baseball. "The Big Hurt" Thomas hit two solo homers against Santana and we won 2–0. Scott assured me my performance of dethroning Johan and his Twins had cemented my dominance in the minds of all the major league teams. We won that series and finally got to the second round of the playoffs after getting knocked out in the first round for four straight years.

I was scheduled to start game one of the ALCS against the Detroit Tigers at home in Oakland. I went into that game still high off the buzz of beating Johan. But as had happened many times before, fear of not maintaining my success caused the wheels to come off the bus again. In just over three innings against the Tigers, I gave up seven hits and five runs. We got swept in four games straight that series, ending our season on a very low note.

My year wasn't bad at 16–10 with a 3.83 ERA, but by this stage of my career, looking back, my lack of humility was the cancer eating away at my life. The irony was while I worked hard to not come off like an egomaniac and always managed to be kind and caring for people, inside my conflicted mind, my pride was fighting hard for dominance.

Toward the end of the season, I had started watching the Mark Wahlberg–produced HBO show called *Entourage*. The main character was Vince "Vinnie" Chase, a Hollywood actor party boy. Like so many young men in their twenties at that time, I wasn't just fascinated with Vinnie Chase; I wanted to *be* Vinnie Chase. But I felt like I had a real chance of living out that fantasy, because like the TV character, I *was* an LA guy and frequented all the same restaurants and nightclubs portrayed on the show. Also, I was about to become a national news story with my upcoming contract that was sure to give my Hollywood status a strong surge. With all of this swirling around inside my ego, I decided I wanted to be single during my once-in-a-lifetime free agent off-season.

I arrived home after the playoffs, and Cassandra was waiting in her car outside my LA house. Even though I had made up my mind to end the relationship, I just couldn't bring myself to have the talk on the first night. We hadn't seen each other in a while and we needed to catch up. But unable to hold in my feelings any longer, the next morning I began explaining to her how everything in my life was about to drastically change because of signing a huge contract soon. The truth was, even though my baseball life played a major role in my decision, I was not totally honest with her about why I wanted to be single.

Sadly, Cassandra didn't see a breakup coming at all. She began crying, at times uncontrollably, so I started crying too. She wept because her heart had just been unexpectedly broken, but I cried because I knew I was hurting someone I loved. We were in and out of tears for many hours that day, talking out the same things over and over.

No matter how many times I broke up with a girl, maybe because

I am more sensitive than most athletes, I couldn't stand to see someone in pain. Ending a relationship never got easier for me, always taking a toll on my heart. Finally, after twelve hours of emotion and discussion, Cassandra walked out my door for the last time at 11:00 p.m. that night.

I was so drained from the experience that I hopped in my Rover and headed straight to my parents' house in the Valley. I sat down and told them the entire story. Mom was comforting and understanding, but Dad just let out a big sigh and responded, "Well, Barry, I know this will sound harsh, but you did what you had to do because it was either your life or hers. You either pick your life and what you want or her life and what she wants for you." My father continually reinforced the idea to me that women were nothing more than a distraction, which most certainly contributed to my vicious cycle of baseball and breakups, breakups and baseball.

To make matters worse, Cassandra and I had a one-year anniversary coming up, so a few days later she dropped off all the gifts she had been making me for many months. There were multiple handmade photo albums filled with memories from our year together as well as a special DVD she'd created for me. Now I felt even guiltier about breaking up with her.

The tension inside my own heart was escalating. My identity struggle was not only affecting me now but also creating real pain for those around me.

Free Agency Is an Oxymoron

Once the off-season began, Scott Boras put together "Barry Zito's Free Agent Presentation," a notebook of my stats year by year in comparison to the other top pitchers in baseball. He highlighted how I had gotten my one hundredth win that season in Texas, which was a major milestone with great timing. One hundred down, two hundred to go. When Scott's book was complete, my body of work showed better numbers than some of the league's highest-paid players. I knew in only a matter of months, my life was about to change big-time. So awaiting the offers, I went back to the club scene, dating whom I wanted and racking up big tabs at expensive restaurants.

With a new level of financial freedom coming very soon, I headed down to the famous Rodeo Drive in Beverly Hills to do some shopping with a friend of mine. Just like Vinnie Chase and his entourage, we smoked a joint in my Range Rover in a parking garage and then took the elevator up right next to the Cartier store, the perfect place to flex my money-muscles.

I strutted into the high-class jewelry store and found the coolest watch they had. I then told the woman behind the counter that I was about to sign a huge baseball contract, and if I could get a hefty discount, I promised to wear the piece at my nationally televised press conference. I wasn't concerned about saving money; I just wanted the power to control the transaction. The watch had a price tag of $19,100. After carefully punching on her calculator, she told me $13,760. *Sold!* I walked out with a big-time gold watch and continued my spending spree down Rodeo Drive. Looking back, I know the global brand of Cartier didn't need my endorsement, but my ego had me convinced otherwise.

Just a few weeks into the off-season, free agent Jason Schmidt of the San Francisco Giants signed a three-year deal with the Dodgers for $47 million, putting him over the $15 million per year mark. Since Jason had been injured for much of his career and I had never missed a start, my price tag instantly skyrocketed. Scott began fielding inquiries from multiple teams.

First, the owners of the New York Mets flew in to meet with Scott and me at the Peninsula Hotel in Beverly Hills. Over dinner with the Mets' brass, the large doors from the hotel's private dining room slid open and out walked Tom Hanks and Ron Howard. Scott already knew Ron and introduced him and Tom to all of us. The Mets' owner pointed at me and told Mr. Hanks, "Now tell this guy he should be a Met!" Tom, being from Sacramento, responded with, "Bull****, stay with the A's!" We all laughed and found out later that he and Ron were plotting the sequel to that year's smash hit *The Da Vinci Code.* I had been around some stars before but those guys are legends. It was such a cool way to cap off my first official meeting as a major league free agent.

In Dad's effort to play out his own fantasies he always pushed me to be a New York Yankee. Leading up to that free agent off-season, he often told me, "Barry, you can be the king of New York City." And I was ready to go all in with the Yankees, too, but they had just spent almost $30 million to negotiate with Japanese pitcher Kei Igawa. Obviously, the Yanks were out of the running, so we continued entertaining offers.

Next, we flew to Texas to meet with Rangers' owner Tom Hicks in his Dallas mansion. After that, the Seattle Mariners sent their brass down for a meeting back at the Peninsula Hotel in LA. Some of the teams were willing to give me a five-year deal, but Scott and I wanted a seven-year to lock up as much time and money as we could. You only get one shot at free agency as a young player, so you have to make the opportunity count.

Throughout the month of December, Scott updated me every few days. He let me know there were a few teams that were willing to pay over $100 million for my services. Hearing those numbers felt like an instant shot of adrenaline in my body, but then simultaneously, deep fear began to stir in me. The familiar demons of expectation were whispering in my ear. So I continued pursuing the distractions that were so readily available in Hollywood.

While Scott was busy negotiating, I focused on training at a facility in Manhattan Beach, California. My Austrian trainer told me about a "mental coach" who had reportedly worked with Jack Nicklaus and Arnold Palmer. Because I was always looking for the next possible angle to advance my career, especially in trying to control my thoughts, I was immediately intrigued. My trainer arranged for him to come down to the gym to meet me.

Andrew was a likable guy and eager to help so we got right to work. He started coming to my house every day and we talked back and forth, long into the night—at his rate of $250 per hour. I soon found out that he had never worked directly with those famous golfers but was only in their periphery somehow. However, since I needed someone close to help calm my fears about all the pressure I'd soon be under, I didn't care.

Andrew led me through the pages of Michael Jordan's and Tiger Woods's books, so I could "absorb the champion energy" from those guys. He also began teaching me how to cultivate my sexual energy to bring more "chi" onto the mound. I looked to the world to solve my problems and was willing to try anything to get what I needed most—a sense of true identity. Back then I was convinced that I could find what I was looking for by achieving greater success in the world, whether from pretty women or pitching dominance.

Before long, Andrew shadowed me everywhere, whether hanging with me at breakfast with friends or in my Rover on road trips. He had me ask a friend of mine if we could use his new home in the Hollywood Hills for a meditation routine, so I did. Andrew and I spent many evenings in deep conversations in the steam shower, and then plunging into the freezing cold outdoor pool. We focused on mantras underwater while holding our breath, and then after resurfacing looked up at the stars and the constellations. He explained their symbolic meaning and how I could draw positive energy from them. I did whatever Andrew asked of me, hoping I could find a way to better shoulder the huge price tag that was about to be placed on my head.

Scott let me know that the San Francisco Giants wanted to meet at our go-to place, the Peninsula Hotel, with owners Peter Magowan and Larry Baer, GM Brian Sabean, and their newly acquired field manager, Bruce Bochy, coming as well. While the meeting went great, there were still negotiations that had to take place. At that point the Mariners were highly interested in a long-term deal for the money we wanted. On the last update, Scott told me he could get the Giants up to $18 million per year. I knew I had some big decisions to make.

Making the choice between Seattle and San Francisco, I had to discuss the decision with Dad, explaining, "You know, I've spent more time in the Bay Area than at my home here in LA. I know the Mariners are offering a lot, too, but I really want to stay where it feels like home. I can also be closer to you and Mom during the season." Dad agreed and allowed me to make the final decision.

The next night, a buddy of mine from high school drove up from San Diego for another Hollywood night on the town. Even though it was just the two of us, I set up a limo for the entire evening and went big, going to Koi, my favorite restaurant. While we were eating, my phone lit up with a text from Scott that read: "7 years at $126M. This will be the highest contract for a pitcher ever. Congratulations, BZ."

Jessica Simpson and her sister, Ashlee, were at the table next to ours. Riding high on my big news, I went over to their group, introduced myself, and invited them all to join us at Teddy's, my favorite LA bar at the iconic Roosevelt Hotel in Hollywood. Although they were surprised that a complete stranger had just invited them out, they politely said they might join me there later.

Now that the contract was a go, Andrew started taking me through in-depth visualizations, telling me I was going to win a Cy Young *and* take the Giants to the World Series in 2007. I was doing my best to believe everything he said. After all, who wouldn't want that? I recorded new affirmations but this time I upped the production level by going to a professional studio and having them lay down specific songs as a soundtrack underneath my words to fire me up.

I had been doing all I could to prepare for the next chapter of my life as the highest-paid pitcher of all time. Counting the days to my big press conference in San Francisco, I planned the perfect trip. I reserved a Hawker 800 from my jet leasing company to accommodate Sally, Mom, Dad, my attorney, and of course Andrew.

After we landed in San Francisco, multiple black sedans with dark-tinted windows pulled up to the plane. My mom looked out the windows in awe, still in shock that she was actually on a private jet. Meanwhile Dad beamed with pride for what we had accomplished. All our years of hard work together culminated in this historic day.

Pulling up to AT&T Park's player lot, I saw fans gathered outside the gates just to get a glimpse of me walking into the stadium. We were greeted by Giants executives and escorted into the tunnel, passing the familiar visiting clubhouse I had known from my years with the A's. I was excited to see the Giants clubhouse for the first time. As my family stayed back in a waiting room, the team trainer met me in front of my new locker room and walked me in.

The wooden lockers were a rich mahogany color and complemented the orange carpet perfectly. Even though it was the off-season, there was one Giants player working out in the gym. He greeted me with a friendly smile and welcomed me to the team. A sign of things to come was that deep down I felt superior to him. After all, because I was the highest-paid pitcher in baseball, I felt like royalty walking through my new home stadium like everyone was just there to be my supporting cast. Since I had never been the center of attention to this extent, I didn't really know how to feel that day. So I just told myself when in doubt, act like a rock star and own it like Vinnie Chase.

After my physical, I was escorted back into the pressroom, where my family had already been seated in the front row. I felt like the man of the hour with the large room full of cameras, reporters, and Giants executives. Suddenly, the chatter and hustle turned to silence. At the long table sat Giants owner Peter Magowan, GM Brian Sabean, and field manager Bruce Bochy. All three had been at our initial free agent meeting at the Peninsula Hotel. I sat down in the empty chair between the owner and GM. As the press conference began, I stared out into the sea of media reps and camera flashes, making sure I kept my promise to the Rodeo Drive store clerk to show off the Cartier watch.

After a couple of questions, Peter Magowan stood up and presented me with my number 75 Giants jersey. I slipped it over my pink button-up and for the next fifteen minutes proceeded to field questions. Cracking a cocky smile, I did my best to appear confident and in control. But inside I was thinking, *How in the world am I worth $126 million?* I was idolized in a way I never had been before. All eyes were on me. Since I always took the credit for my success, I didn't know how to process all the attention. I just did my best to act like this was totally normal for me. But it wasn't. Not at all. On the inside, a storm was raging. That day, fear became my sole motivator.

Big Fear, Bad Form

Just after I signed my deal, Dad's old friend Dick Mills and a widely respected Australian cricket coach named Brent released an instructional book for pitchers. Their core message was that the momentum-based throwing style of cricket could also work well in baseball. They said that old-school pitchers like Koufax used this approach, but over time pitching deliveries had evolved from that particular form.

Since Dad and I had been on a constant quest to increase my velocity, he thought Dick and Brent could help. Just six weeks from my first spring training as the highest-paid pitcher in baseball, need-ing any edge I could get, Dad and I flew to Arizona to work with them. My average velocity at that time was around 87 mph and I felt like I had to get my fastball up into the 90s to justify my contract. As if Scott's presentation of my career stats hadn't been enough.

Working in Dick's backyard, I was awkward at best with the new delivery. They had me take a large step back toward second base and then thrust my body forward in a straight line to the plate. This eliminated my signature big leg kick and extended my stride to the plate by over a foot. Even though my gut told me not to toy with my delivery that had gotten me this far in baseball, I was willing to do anything. And I had made a false idol of velocity for a long time, often feeling jealous of teammates through the years who could "run it up" into the mid-90s. When my session with Dick and Brent was done, Dad encouraged me to bear down for the next six weeks on ingraining the new technique.

So on day one of spring training, with the media circus in full swing, I took to the mound to throw my first bullpen as a Giant. All the writers were watching and TV stations rolling. My new pitching coach, Dave Righetti, was standing right behind me studying closely to see what kind of repertoire the highest-paid pitcher in baseball was featuring. After a couple pitches, Righetti looked shocked and asked me, "What the heck is that?" I responded, "It's momentum pitching, Rags. Still a little new to me, but I'll have it down by the time games start in a couple of weeks."

Honestly, my delivery felt terrible and I could barely throw a strike. Then things got worse once I began throwing my famous Zito curveball. Nowhere to be found, totally flat, not breaking at all. My changeup was horrible too. I really had no idea what I was doing, but I was convinced I was going to be able to throw 95 mph soon. I held on for dear life to the idea that this style change was the right move for my career.

After the first day, the reporters swarmed my locker asking me why I had made such a drastic change in my delivery when coming to a new team with such high expectations. They also explained that Righetti had just expressed his frustration to all of them. He had said my stuff on the mound looked nothing like he had hoped and that he was sure my extra-long stride would flatten out all my pitches. I defended my new delivery to everyone, but the panic was stirring deep inside. My immense lack of self-trust was bubbling to the surface and now as the 126-million-dollar man, there was nowhere to hide.

Trying hard to convince everyone including myself, I told the media, "You don't look at a Michelangelo sculpture halfway done and start commenting on how terrible it is. You wait until the final product." But the reality was certain: I was terrified. I went home plagued by fear that my new delivery could never feel good enough to bring into a real game; fear that my old delivery wasn't enough to meet the huge expectations that were looming. *Both* options were bad, but I finally went with my gut.

I called my father that evening and told him I was done with the momentum pitching and that I needed to revert back to what got me where I was. Dad responded right away, "Barry, I respect that. You gave it your all, and if you feel like you have to go back to your old form, then that's okay."

Just twenty-four hours after unveiling "the new Zito delivery," I felt so relieved to return to my big leg kick and the form that had actually gotten me my contract. But I hated the fact that the Giants coaches and the media had to witness the spectacle in the first place, making a bad first impression. I had proven that I wasn't the seemingly confident pitcher they had signed. As a result, I did my best to explain to everyone, including my teammates, that I had always been open to new methods and how my only goal was to increase velocity. But since the change didn't work, I had no problem giving it up. Everyone was relieved for me to go back to the Zito they had seen pitch in Oakland the past seven years.

Numbers Game

Since my contract was the leading story on all the sports shows, the media was in my face every day with questions like, "Barry, are you nervous about the money? Are you worried about the pressure? How good of a season do you feel will justify the money?" I was lying through my teeth every time, playing it down with a smile, laughing, and answering, "No, I'm not worried at all."

I felt like my every move was under a microscope. Throwing a baseball was once the thing I loved to do more than anything else, yet now it was becoming something I *had* to do perfectly to fend off all the negativity. Like a dam ready to burst, the weight of the expectations was building up by the day. I felt the life getting sucked out of the game.

Fielding all the attention and media scrutiny, as I was getting ready to head into this new season of my life, I better understood what Giants GM Brian Sabean had told me just four weeks earlier right after I had signed my contract. His private warning was beginning to make total sense.

Pulling me aside away from the brass, media, and my family after the press conference, Brian said, "Hey Z, you might as well tattoo that [expletive] number on your forehead."

A bit shaken, I asked, "You mean the $126 million?"

He responded, "Yep. From now on that's all you're ever going to be in people's eyes."

9

Trying Everything, Getting Nowhere

"I allowed the seriousness of things to creep into my mind. The city. The contract. The fans. My new teammates. I wasn't a blue-collar Oakland guy anymore."
—My interview in the *New York Times*[1]

T wenty-foot ceilings.

Marble floors.

Imported Italian doors.

Panoramic view over a private mountain range.

Next door to Muir Woods National Park, home to hundreds of acres of towering redwood trees.

The property had the exact "baller status" amenities I wanted.

Since my Hollywood Hills home was fully remodeled with every detail perfect for my taste, and with an even bigger paycheck on the way, I was ready to own a rock star home in northern California, too, after renting for many years. The Bay Area is as gorgeous as any place in the world, so after touring a number of properties from the city to the suburbs, I decided on a home in Kentfield, a high-end neighborhood in Marin.

When I first saw the home with my real estate agent I was

amazed by the beauty. Within an hour, I called my accountant and asked if I could afford the six-thousand-square-foot villa. Getting the green light, I knew I had found the perfect place to match my growing Bay Area celebrity status.

In January 2007, after the Giants' promotional gathering called Fan Fest had ended, I chartered a private jet to fly to the Sundance Film Festival with some friends. I wanted a final round of Hollywood fun before I had to get fully focused on the upcoming season. While there, I met an actress named Lisa. I remembered hearing her name back when we both attended USC. We made a connection and dated throughout that entire season. Little did I know when we met how her steady companionship would be a comfort to me that year.

Although my new jaw-dropping home satiated my ego, unfortunately, living there didn't help me pitch any better. In my first two games, I gave up ten runs and started my highly anticipated debut season as a Giant with back-to-back losses.

Still struggling to gain any ground in my life, I put Andrew, my "mental coach," on retainer for twenty-four-hour access. He was with me in Arizona during spring training and then rented his own beach house in the Bay Area to be close by for the season. At night, we meditated in my pool and watched the stars. I even installed a steam shower at my Marin home so we could continue all the exercises we had done during our deep talks in LA.

The pattern in my life was that as soon as I saw something wasn't working, I ended it. I was always chasing the quick hit of satisfaction, and when something didn't produce, I moved on, whether drugs, women, or any kind of coach or expert.

Following those first disappointing games at home, the team headed down to San Diego for the next series. Andrew called to inform me that I'd be better off by bringing him on road trips as well. Up to this point I had agreed each time Andrew wanted to further encroach on my life. But when he asked to travel with the team, as only a player's wife might, I snapped out of the spell I had let him put me under all those months. Somehow in that moment I was able to see with a clear perspective that Andrew was conning me all along. I called and fired him the next day.

When I told a close friend of mine that I wasn't working with Andrew anymore, he responded, "Barry, I honestly can't believe you let that strange guy ride your coattails as long as you did." In hindsight, I couldn't believe I had let someone play me the way he had. Reminds me of an old quote: "Those who stand for nothing will fall for anything." The Andrew story was yet another example of my destructive cycle of putting something or someone up on the altar as an idol only to take them down and find something new to which I could bow.

No matter what I tried, I couldn't find any consistency on the mound those first few months. In the bad games, I was booed much more aggressively than even during my worst games in Oakland. Although I had some great years across the Bay, I had zero credibility with San Francisco fans and had to earn *every* cheer. After tough games, I went back to the mansion, only to hear my lone footsteps echo through the marble hallways. I spent many hours alone in my backyard hot tub, racking my brain for solutions to my pitching woes. I was totally miserable. While I could run away from the fans and media to my new mountain hideaway, I could never escape myself. The self-condemning thoughts were *always* with me.

The Other Barry

That season, I became friends with superstar Barry Bonds. I had been assigned the locker closest to his, with a few empty ones between ours allowing plenty of space. Barry B had his own TV set up in his corner, so I watched whatever he had on before games.

Back in spring training, because we were always being hunted down by the media, he had some funny T-shirts made up for us that read, "Don't Ask Me, Ask Barry." People had their own opinions of Barry B back then, but ever since I played with the A's, we always had a special connection.

One eye-opening conversation with him made me rethink my real estate decisions. Since he was one of the greatest players of all time and also very intelligent, I routinely picked Barry's brain. In talking about money and the lifestyle that sports allowed us, he explained why he leased a regular, small apartment during the season. Having no idea that I had just dropped $8 million on a new home, he talked about how important it was to have a place that wasn't so nice that you could just sit back and relax there all day. Barry B didn't want his in-season home to tempt him to get comfortable, but just be a simple space to eat and sleep so he wanted to go back to the field and get to work.

I remember swallowing hard when he told me his philosophy, which from my experience sounded spot-on. Back in the minor-league days I couldn't wait to leave my crappy apartment and get to the field; funny how different I felt about my Marin villa. Like Barry B said, my home was so gorgeous that at times getting in the car and driving for an hour to the field took real effort. If that first year with the Giants I had lived in a humble apartment like the one Sally and I had shared for so long, I might have had a much easier time getting focused for my games. The *other* Barry was dead-on in his mentality. But I still didn't make any changes.

Wide-Awake Nightmare

By mid-June, I was 6–6. One day, right after I had given up a bunch of runs against the A's, GM Brian Sabean called me into his office in the clubhouse. He said, "Barry, I want you to know you're doing fine. You're throwing the ball well but just not getting any breaks. Don't put too much pressure on yourself, okay?" That sort of reassurance was not common to hear from the higher-ups. I'm not sure why Brian gave me that pep talk, but I probably wasn't aware of how much everyone on the team could see what a highly stressed-out mess I was.

The worse I played, the less I wanted to show my face anywhere in the Bay Area. With Barry Bonds approaching retirement, I had been brought in as the "new face of the franchise." The expectation created a fear in me of living amongst all the fans in the hustle and bustle of San Francisco. Had I somehow sensed the struggles that were to come? Had I bought my mountain hideaway only to isolate from everyone who expected so much of me? The truth was I had loved living in San Francisco all those years before but now wanted nothing to do with the city.

During the three-day all-star break the Giants asked me to stay in town and make appearances at a special booth for the game, which was hosted in San Francisco that year. But I refused and decided to go back home to LA. No easy choice, I had to go with the lesser of the two evils. My growing shame was becoming too great to endure, even with just a few hours of facing die-hard baseball fans. And especially since I should have been playing *in* that all-star game on my home field.

My father was not supportive of this decision and wanted me to capitalize on any chance to become more "visible" publicly. He was pushing my publicist hard that year to secure local endorsements and commercials to capitalize on my growing Bay Area status. But I pleaded with him that my priorities needed to be *on the field*. Realizing I was having a very difficult time, he finally agreed that I should stay home in LA to focus on my pitching performance.

All my affirmation recordings that I still listened to regularly, as well as the pages upon pages of "spiritual mind treatments" I was writing, weren't helping me. My declarations of "I am one with the universe" and "I claim pitching greatness" became just empty words, void of their once proven power to transform my performances. *Nothing* was working.

Many restless nights I got up out of bed and paced the cold marble floors in my home. Half asleep yet fully mesmerized by the bright moonlight that shined through the massive windows, for just a moment I'd forget about everything and feel totally calm. But seconds later reality collided with my thoughts to remind me I was being crushed under the weight of my contract. I remember thinking, *Is* this *real life? Am I actually getting paid all this money to pitch like crap? Do I really have to go back to the field tomorrow and face thousands of people booing me?* Watching me from the outside, I had everything I ever dreamed of: a successful career and multimillion-dollar mansions. But I would have traded *all* the stuff for any form of inner peace and security.

My teammates knew I was working hard and doing everything I could to perform at my best. But human nature kicks in when the worst player on the team is making the most money. While everyone acted normal and treated me with respect, I knew they had to be hoping I would soon start pitching like the guy everyone had seen dominate in Oakland. While some athletes could use fear as a powerful personal motivator, I always crumbled under its weight.

I finished 2007 at 11–13, my first losing season, meaning more losses than wins. My ERA was 4.53. One of the reasons I had gone with the Giants over the Mariners was because in the National League you have one less hitter to face since the pitcher is always in the batting lineup. Technically, this should make the National League "easier" than the American League, because in the AL they use designated hitters. Another factor in my decision was that San Francisco's ballpark was known as a "pitcher's park," meaning hitting home runs there was tough to do.

Evaluating the season, I started thinking, *How would I have pitched playing somewhere else?* Even these clear advantages I'd had didn't help me perform any better, which explains even more why Giants fans were not at all happy with their big-money pitcher after year one of the contract.

Chasing Perfection

As the 2007 off-season began, I had to make some repairs to the LA house. Needing a place to stay, I decided to go big and once again throw down the gauntlet on being relevant in Hollywood. I invited Lisa, the actress I was dating, to join me when I rented a famous bungalow at the Chateau Marmont in West Hollywood for thirty days at close to a thousand bucks a night. If other people's bucket lists were to stay there for a weekend, then I decided to live there for a month. The hotel's hedonistic reputation is famous for many Hollywood scandals and for being where the A-listers go to get away from the paparazzi.

Being incognito in LA, I wanted to experience life at the Chateau for myself while escaping the reality that was looming in San Francisco. Since I didn't play for their home team, people in Hollywood weren't really aware of my failed season and just saw me as a successful professional athlete.

After my month off at the Marmont, I began working out as diligently and dedicated as ever. Looking toward the next year, I knew I had to prove my first season was just a fluke. My plan for year two of the seven-year contract was to show everyone that I was worth the big money. What felt like determination on the surface was more like sheer panic underneath.

By now, the Cy Young felt like a curse as I was haunted by the thought of *How will I ever get back to dominating like I had done in 2002?* But nothing could live up to that record year. Just as my first win in the big leagues had created the "299 to go" response from Dad, now his "one Cy Young down and *nine* more to go" was messing with my head too.

Added to that dynamic was the realization that my "creative mind," Eastern religions, and "mental coach" applications were all coming up empty. One teaching was telling me to *lose* all attachment to desires, while another was telling me to focus intently on *exactly* what I desired. I didn't know *what* to think anymore. I was always trying to find the winning formula in a new book, but it was nowhere to be found. Anything that appeared to work for a while soon failed me. My trips to Barnes & Noble became more frequent than ever, as I scanned the self-help section once again for answers.

But every belief system and metaphysical solution I tried eventually failed because they never got me away from the root of the problem: *myself.* While I was the cause of all my own turmoil, no matter the method, they all taught basically the same thing—if I was headstrong enough, I could be my own savior.

Around that same time, something strange began taking place in my games. My performance every five days became an obligation to justify the money, and I felt I had to dominate to do so. So even pitching a decent game was still a huge failure because *decent* didn't justify $126 million. If I did happen to pitch really well, I would not allow myself to feel the joy of the victory, but only the short-lived satisfaction that I had fended off the fans' anger for one more day.

Amid this mental turbulence, I could see only one way out: keep searching for the magic formula. So I kept pushing.

It Takes a Village

The fans were already frustrated with me before I even threw my first pitch of the 2008 season, and things only got worse from there. My first game against the Dodgers I gave up four runs in five innings. Loss. Then Milwaukee, five runs in five innings. Loss. Then against St. Louis, four runs in six innings. Loss. The next game, four runs in six innings. Loss. Next game, five runs in three innings. Loss. Five games into the season, I had the worst record in the Major Leagues with an ERA of 5.61.

Getting ready to face Cincinnati at home, Dad came to stay with me to go back through the *Creative Mind* book once again. I actually recorded all those sessions, because I knew with his getting older, I would need them if he passed away. Before my next game, in my hat I drew a stick figure pitcher surrounded by a bunch of dots going up to the sky. During the game, I would look in my hat and remind myself that I was immersed in "the universal mind," trying to access it to dominate the Reds.

But this time Dad's sessions and even the drawing didn't work. I pitched a disastrous three innings and gave up eight runs that day. Following the game, Bochy called me into his office. My next start was supposed to be the following weekend in Philadelphia. He said, "Hey, Barry, I know it's not easy for you out there right now, and I think we need to give you a breather. We're going to skip your start in Philly and put you in the bullpen for three games. A little reset might help break things up a bit. Once we head to Pittsburgh after the Phillies series, we'll plug you back into the rotation to make your next start."

The missed game in Philadelphia was the first one of my career. Not due to a physical injury, but more like a mental injury. That entire series, the hovering Philly fans screamed all kinds of obscenities down at me as I sat in the bullpen. I did improve some in my next start at Pittsburgh with five innings and two runs, but we still lost. By now, I had no wins and seven losses.

The real estate agent who had sold me my home in Hollywood saw what was going on with my season and called. She said she knew Tony Robbins, the life coach who had authored multiple best-sellers, and made arrangements for him and me to meet and talk in a hotel room in San Francisco. Working with me at no charge, Tony just wanted to help in any way he could. He gave me his very best motivational talk, and by the time he was done, I was pumped! It was always easier for me to feel confident when a coach reminded me that I was a good pitcher. The next couple of days, Tony and I talked on the phone several times. His goal was to fill up my empty tank just like he had done with thousands of other successful people.

My next start was at home against Houston. Feeling inspired by Tony's life coaching, I pitched six innings, allowing just three runs. Even though our team lost, for the first time in eight starts I didn't get credit for the loss. The next game against the White Sox, I labored through 110 pitches in five innings, giving up just two runs, but took the loss anyway. Our team didn't have a great offense but that was no excuse for my poor performances. I was now 0–8 with a 6.25 ERA.

That week, a sportswriter released an article comparing my stats and $14 million salary for the year to the other highest-paid pitchers in the league. There was *no* comparison with all the other guys who had all gotten off to great starts. To add insult to injury, he also threw in some nasty comments about me. But amazingly, my team-mates had my back. They pinned the article up in the locker room and scribbled their own "thoughts" across the page, defending me. Several guys told me they wouldn't give that writer any more inter-views for a while, basically boycotting him. With zero self-worth, I felt so good to get that kind of support from the guys.

That May after a home game on my thirtieth birthday, I ended up without a car at the field, so teammate Matt Cain offered to give me a ride home. A couple of hours later when we pulled into my driveway at the Marin home, there was a large crowd of people wait-ing outside. My actress girlfriend, Lisa, had put together a surprise party for me. My family, Bay Area friends, LA friends, and the majority of my teammates were there, about sixty people in all. Even the veteran players had taken the time to drive an hour out of the city up to my house. In my fragile mental state, I was convinced that everyone on the team was disgusted with me since I was making more money than they were and hurting the team every five days. Having them show up for my birthday, I got emotional and held back tears as I was thanking them all for coming.

I was still creating "spiritual mind treatments" that I recorded with classical music in the background. Some of them were thirty minutes long, proclaiming how successful I was. But there was now one major issue: I no longer believed *any* of what I was saying about myself. The affirmations started to sound more like lies. I didn't really throw 93 mph and I wasn't the best pitcher in the league. All in just year two of a *seven-year* contract.

One day during the season, a delivery truck showed up at my house. Dad had ordered a pitching mound, net, and radar gun for me to set up in the backyard of the Marin home. He advised, "Barry, just get out there and get back to work."

I responded, "But Dad, I throw my bullpens at the field. This is the middle of the season!"

But listening to my father's coaching, I started going out and throwing *before* I went to the field—to throw. When a player starts to perform poorly, a lot of people assume they are slacking off and being lazy. But for me, I was probably working *too* hard. I was putting in too many reps on the mound. I felt like I was on one side of the room and my lifelong pitching skills were on the other with a brick wall dividing us. I knew my ability was there but I couldn't access it to save my life.

I had heard about a book that Oprah was endorsing. The concept was very Eastern and, of course, I got it and devoured the pages as quickly as I could. Feeling confident in this new truth, I went out against the Marlins and pitched six innings and gave up just one run. By late May, I had finally gotten my first win of the year.

On June 25, I was 2–11 with a 6.32 ERA and about to start in Cleveland. I decided for that game I just wanted to enjoy the feeling of the ball coming off my fingers like I had felt in long toss. Before the game, I had the idea to get a blank sheet of paper and draw out a grid of squares. Nine rows down, one for each hitter in the lineup, and four columns across, one for each time that hitter came to bat; my own version of a scorecard. I filled in the names of the opposing lineup and at the very top I wrote a mental slogan to focus on. For example, "Well-timed delivery and a crisp release off the fingertips." The goal was to concentrate on what *I* was doing and not what the *hitters* were doing.

As I came off the field after each inning, I pulled the scorecard out of my jacket pocket and next to each hitter I placed either a big check mark or a large "X." The check was if I was aggressive and trusted myself on the pitch. The "X" was if I doubted myself and was afraid of a bad result. At the end of each game, I added up the Xs and check marks to see how well I executed my own criteria, outside of the game's results. The concept allowed me to keep myself accountable for what I could control, to not allow myself to doubt and become obsessive on what happened after I released the ball. I decided to keep using my new "personal scorecard" for increased focus, no matter how I pitched.

Seeing that I was searching for answers, a veteran teammate recommended a spiritual healer from LA named Paul who he felt had helped him improve his performance. Paul had been a competitive swimmer in New Zealand and looked a lot like the pictures I'd seen of Jesus with long flowing hair, piercing eyes, and a gentle face. Tall and lanky, Paul was a laid-back surfer dude like myself, so I liked him right away. He also had an Olympic gold medal, which was impressive. Unlike most macho guys in the sports world, Paul reminded me of my old coach Rick Peterson, sensitive and not afraid to be transparent about his feelings.

Paul flew to San Francisco, and I met him in a hotel room before a home game. After we talked for a while, upon his instruction, we knelt on the carpet and he told me to breathe in as deeply as I could, then exhale forcefully, then in again, then out. After five breaths, Paul had me hold my inhale as long as I could, then rise up onto my knees, fully arch my back, and force my air out as fast as possible while making an audible "Ahhhhh" sound as I did.

I was hit with such an intense head rush that I immediately blacked out. A few seconds later, lying facedown on the carpet, I came to and assumed I must have passed out. Seeing how freaked out I was, Paul spoke to me in a tranquil manner and reassured me I was fine. After returning to full consciousness, I felt like I had gone into another realm, reminiscent of the LSD trips from my teen years, except I was totally sober now. Although scary, the euphoria was amazing and I was highly intrigued. I believe it had something to do with depriving my brain of oxygen and creating some altered state as a result.

Later when I got to the clubhouse, owner Peter Magowan was holding a meeting with the team. I slipped in and sat down on the floor in the back still feeling the effects of the breathing exercises with Paul. With that first session, I was sold and hired him to start coaching and meeting with me on a regular basis.

At the all-star break in July, my agent, Scott, arranged for me to go visit famed sports psychologist and author of *The Mental Game of Baseball*, Harvey Dorfman, at his home in Asheville, North Carolina. Dad and I had read his book throughout my childhood. Harvey had worked with some of the greatest ballplayers in history. I spent three days there, talking with him for eight to nine hours a day.

In his crotchety voice, like Mickey from the Rocky movies, Harvey told me, "You think it's all about you, huh? So those fans go to bed every night with Barry Zito on their minds? Well, I hate to break it to you, but they don't care about you! It ain't about you! These people have enough problems in their own lives. They're not thinking about yours." Harvey used a bit more colorful language, but you get the idea. He was delivering a reality check and a wake-up call all at the same time. And oddly, I loved his abrasive honesty. In my world of soft-spoken spiritual gurus, I had never been talked to like that before.

I was pitching so poorly that I hid down in our dugout during our games while my teammates leaned out over the top rail and cheered for the team. If I became visible to the fans, the verbal abuse would start up. One night I got the courage to get up there and a group of college-age guys started ragging me: "Zito, you are the absolute worst pitcher ever!" I could only play it off for so long and after a couple of innings retreated back into the clubhouse, grabbed my cell phone, and slipped into a bathroom stall to call my mom with my eyes full of tears. Knowing I was in a game, Mom picked up as I quietly told her what happened and how I felt. Sometimes in moments like this, I thought I was going completely insane. She comforted me as always, just listening as I vented and cried.

After the call on that particular night with the college guys, I tried something I had never done before in an effort to quiet the trash-talkers. *Kill 'em with kindness.* I told the clubhouse attendant to take them hot dogs and beers with the message, "These are on Zito." When I returned to the dugout, I got back up on the rail and when they saw me, those same guys started yelling, "Thanks, Zito! You are the man!" I was always baffled at how fans could change their tune so quickly. Maybe Harvey was right and it wasn't about me at all?

That summer was up and down on the field. A good game followed by two bad ones. My pitching performances were just as inconsistent as my spiritual approaches. The only part of the day that I enjoyed was when I was alone in my home. Once I pulled up to the field, I wrapped myself with an emotional armor to make it through another day. Getting booed while standing in the outfield shagging batting practice made me think I would have been better off re-signing with the A's back in 2006. Since I had no credibility with Giants fans and had started pitching poorly from day one, they were all angry with me.

I wasn't the savior the Giants fans were hoping for, but instead became the sacrificial lamb.

P90X and After-Parties

By August, Lisa told me she felt we needed a break. She wanted to take a week off from the relationship to "get some space." Taken off guard, I still agreed. But the week apart brought a surprise realization for me. I was in Atlanta on a road trip and we had planned to talk on the phone. The seven days had given me a strong sense that the relationship was actually over, so I let Lisa know. That wasn't at all what she was expecting, but "the space" had allowed me to consider my own feelings. We broke up that day.

Having some bandwidth back in my life and with my buddy Barry Bonds gone from the team, I struck up a friendship with Brian Wilson. Brian had made the all-star team his first year as the closer. He was very self-assured, covered in tattoos, and fully dedicated to baseball and working out.

I finished the 2008 season with an abysmal record of 10–17 with a 5.15 ERA. Just before the off-season began, I asked Brian if he wanted to move into my Hollywood home with me. He agreed and took over Sally's old room. She had moved out, and in her own words told me, "to preserve the purity of our dynamic of big sister and little brother." Brian was very intelligent, uniquely funny, and quite headstrong. Being around someone who had such an unshakable belief in his own skills as he did was inspiring. And since I was deeply insecure as a baseball player, I wanted to show off to Brian that I was still an all-star in the Hollywood club scene.

We got up every morning and did P90X and then played long toss on a dirt road that sprawled across a nearby canyon. My nutritionist dropped off perfectly engineered meals for us each night for the next day. I was losing body fat and getting stronger than I had ever been. Most nights, we still went out to the clubs to meet girls and had a great time together. Regardless of how late we got in, we were back in the garage ready to work out the next morning, always keeping each other accountable for our baseball goals.

Brian and I were getting closer and enjoying all sides of our experience together. One night in a club I pulled him aside and said, "Weez, I love you like a brother and as long as I am single, you and I will live together." I just felt better with him around, and I wanted him to know he could always call my place home.

When Brian and I were out, my buddy Josh the promoter often came over to ask me if I wanted to have an "after prom," meaning invite an exclusive group from the club to my house after closing time. The nights I agreed, Brian and I left the club around 1:00 a.m. to go to the liquor store, stock up, and then head to my house where we would ice everything down and get the music pumping. We paid the bouncer at the club to come work at my front door to keep the stragglers out. By around 2:30 a.m., people began to arrive at my place.

While the party usually broke up by 5:00 a.m., there were many mornings that I got up and came into my living room only to find some guy I didn't know still there. Some of the celebrities that came to my house in those days were Leonardo DiCaprio, Scarlett Johansson, Lindsay Lohan, and the Hilton sisters. Several nights, paparazzi camped out in front to get pictures as people left. Sometimes the next day, one of my friends would name a celebrity that was at my house the night before, but I often never saw them or even knew they were there.

The rampant partying wasn't the only thing I did to uphold my image off the field in 2008. During that season, the owner of the popular clothing company True Religion contacted my publicist. He had seen my photo and wanted to hire me to be their fall campaign model with the world famous Bar Refaeli being the female model. Following the baseball season, we did the shoot in Malibu. I had no idea at the time that my photo would end up being posted on billboards and buses across Japan and Europe, and even in my own downtown San Francisco. For working models, this was a once-in-a-lifetime opportunity, but for me, it was just another way to distract myself from my tanking career.

That 2008 off-season I also discovered another distraction, albeit a more expensive one. I bought a 2006 Ford GT, black with silver racing stripes that was jaw-dropping gorgeous. I drove that dream car all around Hollywood in an effort to regain the sense of success I hadn't felt in so long. Through the next few years, I also purchased some other bucket list vehicles to boost my self-worth: a black Audi R8 Spyder, a Mercedes E63 Sedan, and even a black McLaren MP4. Although they were incredibly exciting to own and drive, they never filled the hole in my soul.

While 2008 was a disastrous season on the field, I made sure I had a Cy Young–caliber season *off* the field. I also succeeded in establishing myself once again as "The Man" who wore the coolest clothes, drove the fastest cars, and threw some of the wildest parties in Hollywood. I was making sure to check *all* the boxes I could.

Enter Amber

A wealthy buddy of mine, Kevin, had texted to invite me to his luxury box at Dodger Stadium to watch the LA Madonna concert. Another of my many Hollywood acquaintances was a short Italian man that we had nicknamed "The Model Wrangler." Everywhere this guy went an interchangeable string of models followed behind. While we were watching the concert, the door flew open and in walked the "Wrangler," followed by a literal line of girls, all totally decked out in their best club dresses and high heels.

Introducing myself to the models, when I got to one of the girls, she seemed to light up. Everything about her just shined with a unique glow. She had such genuine warmth. I was immediately taken with her. With all the countless beautiful girls I had met over the years, I had never had that kind of love-at-first-sight sensation. I immediately thought to myself, *Whoa! What is* this? *Something is different about this one.*

"Hi, I'm Amber," she said.

"Great to meet you, Amber. I'm Barry Zito."

Amber was obviously not a California girl. She had the blonde hair and blue eyes common in my home state, but there was something different about her that I had never encountered before. Not only was she more beautiful than any model-actress I had met, she had an inner assuredness that was equally as gorgeous.

"So where are you from, Amber?" I asked.

Smiling ear to ear she replied, "I'm from Oran, Missouri, a tiny farm town of 1,236 people—but 1,235 since I'm out here in California."

I felt something new in my heart, like a deep sense of confirmation. As she spoke, I sensed this inner light beaming through her. In a matter of seconds, I went from confident Hollywood bachelor to a jelly-legged, nervous mess. I did all I could to be cool, but couldn't believe what was happening. Ever since I started liking girls, I had wanted to settle down one day with a young lady from the Midwest or the South. I had been to those parts of the country for baseball tournaments in high school and college and was always impressed with how women there carried themselves.

The more we talked, the easier it became, like we were the only ones in the room. When Amber laughed, she crinkled her nose in this most perfect way, so I tried to keep her laughing throughout the entire night. She also had a Marilyn Monroe–type beauty mark on her upper lip that was the icing on the cake. This girl was *perfect*.

But toward the end of the concert, Amber threw me a curveball when she mentioned she was dating someone. After the show ended and we all walked out to our cars, I went over and asked if she would like to join us at a club. She smiled graciously and politely declined my offer. But somehow, I still managed to get her phone number.

Over the next year, I randomly texted Amber, while always being careful to respect that she had a serious boyfriend. But even when I tried to just meet her for coffee as a friend, she was always too busy. *Every* time. Finally one day, she reached out and asked about my autographing some baseballs for her family who were big fans of the game. Right away, I thought this was finally going to be my opportunity to meet up.

When I tried to invite her to my house for the autographs, she politely asked, "Is there a way maybe you could just mail them to me? I'm superbusy right now so it's going to be hard for me to find any time. I would really appreciate it." I finally gave in to the tough conclusion that Amber and I were only going to be long-distance friends. But! . . . If she ever did become single, I knew I was going to work hard to win her over.

You Just Have to Surrender

As my baseball career was tanking, I was also dealing with my parents' failing health. Mom was not doing well. While her liver transplant had been successful in extending her life, the medication she had to take each day to prevent her body's rejection of the organ constantly compromised her immune system. That also led to her getting a cancerous tumor the size of a golf ball behind her right eye in 2003. She had gone to a specific doctor in Mexico for his help, and while the cancer was finally cured, she continued to deal with multiple health issues. The hospital where she and Dad went for treatment for various things over the years was a few miles south of the Mexican border.

In 2008 Mom became very ill again and checked back into that same hospital. That September during a road trip to San Diego to play the Padres, I went to Mexico to visit her. As she and I were alone in her room, Mom began to cry and opened up to me in a way she never had before. She shared, "Barry, I have been battling these health issues for so many years and I just can't handle the pressure anymore of having to create my own experience. Trying to force my mind to think positively is so difficult when I am constantly being bombarded by physical pain and the reality that my body is not well. I can't sleep at night and everything hurts. I don't know what to do, Barry. I feel so hopeless."

In support of my pitching struggles, Mom had bought me a cross necklace earlier that season that had the word *surrender* etched on it. Calling upon some concepts I had recently read in a spiritual teaching called *A Course in Miracles*, I blurted out the best thing I knew to say: "Mom, you just have to surrender. Let God take over and take the pressure off. Tonight when you go to sleep, just surrender and give it up to God. Let Him take it all."

I ended up staying and spending the night in an adjoining room. The next morning when I woke up and went in to see her, Mom was beaming and reported, "Barry, you'll never guess what happened last night. I had the best night's sleep ever. I gave it all to Jesus. I told Him I don't want this anymore, so take it. . . . I surrendered. . . . Wow, Barry, who ever thought after pastoring our metaphysical church my whole life that *I* would become a Christian? It feels so good to give everything in my life to God."

Within a few weeks, Mom got so sick in that Mexican hospital that they called my sister Bonnie to come get her. Her body was riddled with infection. Bonnie drove Mom back up to Cedars-Sinai in LA where she had undergone the liver transplant. Her final days were spent there. My conversation with Mom was near the end of my season in September, and she died in November with Sally and me by her side.

Just like when the liver disease almost killed her, Dad wasn't there because he was in denial as to how sick she was. He always believed his positive affirmations would work and she would come home healthy. Right after Mom passed, Sally and I went to Dad's house to deliver the news. He couldn't quite believe what we were saying, that she was actually gone. His spiritually based denial was challenged for the first time by the reality of his own wife's death.

While at that time I did not understand the biblical concepts of salvation, redemption, and what Christ accomplished on the cross, miraculously, the right words came out of my heart to Mom's spirit. Being the pastor of a metaphysical church all her life, my mother would never have admitted she was a sinner or needed Jesus as her Savior. I never even heard the word *sin* in our house, and Mom always referred to Jesus as merely an example of perfect mental mastery. She would tell us that if we used our minds the right way, we could all be our own individual Christs. But that night and the next day, something was vastly different. Mom had a new sense of humility. As she spoke, she was talking about the Jesus of the Bible, the Savior who died on the cross and rose again for our salvation. Mom was clear in her confession. I believe with all my heart she invited Christ to come into her life that night.

But after my mother's funeral, I hit the ground running, right back into my normal, crazy lifestyle. I didn't allow myself to grieve, which is always a mistake for anyone when a loved one passes.

No changes. No difference. Somehow even my own words of Christ and surrender didn't faze me.

Nobody's Fault but Mine

"It's a team effort to get to this place. But I stand behind
Boch. He's the skipper. I stand behind his decision."

—My statement, 2010 playoffs press
conference, *NBC News*[1]

Hey man. I know this sounds crazy but I'm having this strong desire
to choke someone right now. Feeling really aggressive."

While keeping my phone hidden in my lap under the table-
cloth edge I texted my roommate, best friend, and teammate Brian
Wilson. We were out on a double date at a nice restaurant, and I
didn't want the girl I was with to see what I was doing.

"What? Choke someone? Dude, that's not like you. You okay?"
Brian texted me back and then stared across the table at me with a
what's-up-with-you look on his face. I just gave him a quick shrug
and tried to act normal with my date.

Welcome to the Jungle

The strange feeling was likely the result of a crazy experiment I got in
on when one of my spiritual practitioners offered me a homeopathic

remedy to connect me with my "spirit animal." You probably figured spirit animals would enter the picture at some point, right? After assessing me over the phone, the scientist declared mine to be a lion. He gave me some tablets to take that he said contained real lion's milk. I never asked him how you milk a lion but I often wondered.

After several days on "the milk," Brian and I were on the double date when the thoughts of choking someone began to overwhelm me. As a normally chill, laid-back guy, this was completely out of character for me. A couple of hours later while still out on the town, a friend of mine saw me and asked if I would come next door to grab a drink at the bar where she worked. I gladly agreed.

Excusing myself from Brian and the girls, my friend took me down the street and brought me in through the back door of the very crowded bar. As she was leading me through, a guy approached and my friend yelled over the loud music, "Barry, I want to introduce you to my boss." As I stuck out my hand to shake his, he grabbed me by both shoulders and started frantically shaking me, saying, "Zito! Zito! So great to have you in here, man!"

With my personal space totally violated, rage instantly permeated my body. Reacting out of some sort of primal instinct, I grabbed him by the throat, pinned him to the ground, and in a roaring voice yelled, "Don't you ever grab me like that!" I kept my choke hold on him until he fully submitted. The huge crowd parted around us and we immediately became the focus of everyone in the bar. Realizing the sudden attention, I quickly stormed out the door, now high on adrenaline.

After helping her boss up off the floor, my friend came outside after me and asked what was going on. Then the owner walked out, completely defeated, and said, "Dude! Why'd you have to embarrass me like that in front of my whole bar?" I shook my head, telling him it was not okay to approach a complete stranger like he did. He knew he was in the wrong and apologized for his exuberance. I then made amends with my friend and left. As I walked back to meet Brian, I started wondering why I had reacted in such an aggressive way.

Later at home trying to settle myself down, I called Paul and told him what had happened. After hearing my odd, out-of-character story, he got fired up, which made his accent sound even thicker: "Well, mate, do you know how a lion kills its prey?" He paused for a dramatic effect. "He goes for the throat and chokes 'em out! You're becoming a lion, Barry!"

Paul was obviously referring to the tablets I had been taking. In that moment, my mind rushed back to what I had texted Brian at the beginning of the night about choking someone. Finally connecting the dots, I thought it was obvious the lion's milk had taken effect, because I had *never* wanted to do such a thing before; in fact, violence was always something I avoided.

Whether the catalyst was physical or mental, for my next few games I had more aggression on the mound and I dominated. But always relying only on my own strength and unreliable willpower, what went up had to come down, and my performance quickly fell back to mediocre again. After my short streak, I assumed the lion's milk concoction had lost its potency, so I stopped taking it.

With the brief run of good games and the added confidence of being around Brian, I posted my lowest ERA as a Giant in that 2009 season. But the fix certainly wasn't permanent and proved that I wasn't going to achieve success by trying to be something I wasn't— namely, an aggressive, violent person.

That year Brian and I lived together during spring training in Arizona and then for the season. Even with my home in Marin, we rented a place in my familiar Marina neighborhood. We wanted to be in the middle of the action in the city during home stands. Brian was giving me the confidence I needed on and off the field, always talking me up with encouragement. Becoming like one of my new metaphysical books, I added him to my "coach" list. Brian and I were inseparable as best friends. But even with the constant "bro" connection, I was still meeting with Paul for his inspiration and advice on everything from the girls I dated to my mind-set on the field.

But as Brian kept getting more popular for his performance on the field and my pitching continued to hover in the mediocre range all season, jealousy started to seep into my heart. When we were out at the same hot spots I had frequented back in my Cy Young days, fans were coming up to *him*, asking for his autograph, and ignoring me. While Brian was getting, "Oh my gosh, it's Brian Wilson!" I heard, "Oh hey, Zito, good seeing you man." To his credit, Brian handled all those situations with great care toward me and was always a good friend.

Being around Brian in public eventually became painful for me. Many times when friends would be in town from LA, I opted to stay home alone while they went out on the town. By the end of the season with my ego in full control, I informed Brian that I wanted to live on my own instead of being roomies again, breaking the brotherly promise I had made to him just a year earlier. While I never really gave him a reason why, I tried to make my idea of his getting his own place somewhere in the Hills seem like a good one.

Although Brian didn't let on at the time, I'm sure my decision surprised him. We had such a great time that last year together, and he couldn't have known the real reasons behind my wanting to create space in our friendship. But the decision backfired a bit for me as he began hosting parties at his new place that was just one canyon over from mine in Hollywood. My old entourage was now spending all their time at his place. And I was alone.

The strangest thing I got involved in during that off-season was when Paul told me about a mad scientist he had found in Canada who could trigger new brain growth in adults. The first step was to buy a 24-karat gold bar and send it to him. (Now, stay with me here, people.) In his lab, the scientist fed the gold to microscopic bacteria and, as a result of a process in their digestive system, a new compound was created that could generate human brain tissue. That meant we had to consume the bacteria's, uh . . . excrement. Needless to say, this was not FDA approved.

Paul and I, with a couple other people in tow, flew across the country to the scientist's house. Once there, we put the tablets that were filled with the bacterial excrement from the gold bar under our tongues. Ingesting the pills gave me a strong sense of euphoria that reminded me very much of doing crystal meth as a teenager. We spent the next eight hours "under the influence" with the scientist taking notes and observing us.

Yep, I actually did that.

Flipping the Script

The 2010 season started out in a very strange way. The morning of my first start, I was in my hotel room in Houston overcome with anxiety when I called Paul and made a confession, "I am a mess, man. I am feeling terrible about my game tonight, like I am going to give up eight runs in two innings."

He responded, "Yeah, mate, so what? Let's say you do give up those runs, then what?"

I shot back, "But Paul, I have to pitch great this year, man. I'm in the fourth year of my contract and need to prove myself!"

Then Paul said something that totally clicked. "Barry, okay, since you are unable to control your thoughts, then stop fighting them. If you really are going to pitch terribly tonight, then so be it. Let's just accept them. At least go out there and enjoy actually throwing the baseball."

I knew I couldn't reel myself in from the negative thoughts, so I agreed to try his crazy approach. "Okay, Paul, well, I guess I am going to really suck tonight," I said as we both chuckled.

Thinking negatively *on purpose* was not at all what had been wired into me all those years growing up. But I always listened to whomever was speaking into my life at the time and so I decided to try. I flipped the script and began to visualize hypothetical newspaper headlines about my crappy game. Ironically on the field that first night, the different mind-set took the fear away and removed the intense expectation that was always hanging over me. My mantra going into a game became: "I'm going to suck today." But the systemic problem was that my motivation was built totally on the wrong foundation.

I got the win in Houston, pitching six innings with just three hits and no runs. Playing worst-case scenario seemed to work really well in allowing me to be completely free out on the mound. So well, in fact, that the change led to my best run ever, stats wise, as a San Francisco Giant. Over the next two months, I went 6–1 with a 2.16 ERA. *That's Cy Young Award pace.* The same media personalities that had been on my case for three years were now predicting I would win eighteen games and finally become "the Zito we all expected."

When It's Right, You Just Know

In May, I was scheduled to start a night game against the Cardinals. I remembered that Amber Seyer, the girl I had met at the Madonna concert eighteen months earlier, had rooted for the Cards her entire life. Having surrendered to just being friends, we hadn't spoken in months, so I texted: "Hey, I'm starting against your Cardinals this Saturday. Any chance you and some girlfriends would want to take a road trip up to San Fran and hang? You all can stay at my place if you want." I assumed the response would be another no, but I was determined to keep trying. To my shock and surprise, Amber texted back, "Hey! We might actually do that. I'll let you know soon!" I was *so* pumped I was actually going to get to see Amber in person.

I pitched awesome that night, going eight scoreless innings and beating her home team. After I finished my interviews on the field, while still in uniform I walked up into the tunnel on the way to the clubhouse. There standing with all the players' families was Amber and her friends. I gave her a "hello hug" and rushed into the clubhouse to get cleaned up as quickly as I could so I could go show her around my city.

Amber told me later that when she saw me in the tunnel, she was overcome with a feeling like electricity, much like the one I had the night I met her.

Her friends offered to drive her car so she could ride with me. When we got in, I looked over at her and asked, "So what have you been up to? How's your boyfriend?" Amber answered, "He's good. Well, actually, we broke up." I immediately thought to myself, *Wait! You mean you're single!?* At that moment, over the sound of the angels singing, I vowed to myself, *I am going to marry this girl.* Of course, what actually came out of my mouth was, "Oh, wow, I'm sorry to hear that. Hope you're okay."

The four of us went out and had a great time singing classic songs at my favorite karaoke bar. Later that evening, Amber and I kissed for the first time. The connection was made and soon we began dating. Because of her past relationship, she needed to move slowly, which of course I understood. With my "married to baseball" approach even more instilled after my breakup with Lisa, I had already promised myself that I wouldn't get married until after retirement. But the more time Amber and I spent together, the closer we got and eventually decided to become exclusive.

So, Why Are You Here?

As for my on-field performance, the "I'm going to suck today" didn't have much shelf life either. Check another one off the list. As soon as the hype of everyone's expectations and predictions set in, I started pitching for "them" again. Maintaining mass approval was back on the throne. My mind-set reverted to: "I have got to be *really* good out there today." And so I cratered. The Zito train flew off the tracks *again*, derailing my season. After those magical first six weeks, I won only three of my next twenty-six games, losing thirteen of them and finishing the season at 9–14 with a 4.15 ERA. At 199.1 innings pitched, that was the closest I came to eclipsing the 200-inning mark as a Giant, something I did *six straight years* while in Oakland.

As I spoke about in the introduction, on Sunday, October 3, the final game of the season, the last play of the game, my ex–best friend Brian Wilson was on the mound and we beat the Padres, putting us in the playoffs. The fans went crazy and we all stormed out onto the field. But I knew I had only hurt us and not contributed to the success to now launch us into postseason play. I was the worst pitcher on the team, with the biggest paycheck. My contract number that was "tattooed on my forehead" started to glow like a neon sign that day. As we ran around the field to celebrate the win, with my sunglasses on, my tears falling from underneath weren't from joy, but shame.

Back in the locker room, the difficult conversation with Bochy occurred, informing me I wouldn't be on the playoff roster. That was followed by the even more difficult conversation with my father about my thoughts of quitting the game. Regardless, I was determined to fight through the criticism and the cruelty that was going to undoubtedly come my way. My plan was to stay with the team in the postseason, ready to play if they needed me.

Worn out emotionally, when I finally got home that night I called Paul, my spiritual coach, and told him we were done. Another abrupt ending. I was going to fly solo for a while. After the tough conversation with Dad about my future, I knew it was time to be my own man and work this out alone, with no coach, maybe for the first time ever. Something in me was saying loud and clear to disassociate myself from *anything* that felt remotely like a crutch. And this time, I had to listen.

The next day was the first day of workouts for the playoffs, and of course, the big story for all the sports media was how the Giants' highest-paid player wasn't even on the roster. Avoiding the media onslaught about my globally advertised failure was a great reason for me to retreat back to LA. I told the Giants PR team that I would do *one* interview down in the dugout, not in the locker room. Thirty minutes later, a rep came and told me all the media was gathered outside on the field. He added, "Dude, there are a *lot* of them out there."

I walked out and they were packed tight in a semicircle at four deep with cameras rolling and microphones on. I felt like a prisoner facing the tribunal, knowing the firing squad was loaded and aimed at my heart. The first question was: "So, Barry, being that you aren't eligible to play, what are you doing here?" I offered up only a surface layer of the truth, "Well, it's important for me to stay in shape and support the team in any way I can."

And while my statement *was* the truth, the deeper reality was I was holding on to any remains of my baseball career as tightly as I could. After those twenty very long minutes passed and the media circus finally ended, I jogged out onto the field to throw a bullpen. I was so angry that I took my emotions out on the ball, pitching as hard as I could. My coach had to come watch me throw, but I knew he wanted to be focused on the real playoff starters and not wasting his time on me. My shame just kept piling higher and higher.

Over the years, I had worked with a lot of great players and so many had the innate ability to look at everyone around them and just say, "I don't care what you think. Doesn't matter what you say about me." But as I looked around at everyone, I felt like I was seeing myself through their eyes and their opinions. I felt hollow inside. Not only was I assuming that everyone around me was thinking and saying negative things, I was sure they were right in their assessment. I felt like I was living from the outside in, devoid of any voice inside me that might confirm who I really was, regardless of everyone else's opinions.

After enduring the pain of watching my team in the playoffs, my self-worth plummeted even more when my longtime Giants throwing partner, Matt Cain, told me he was going to start throwing with Madison Bumgarner. Changing throwing partners might not sound like a big deal, but in such a superstitious sport like baseball, keeping your routines consistent and reliable are a huge part of your success. Players almost never alter their daily rituals in fear that they won't be as confident when they step on the field. The only time a player will adjust their routine is when they are struggling and need to "shake things up."

Since Matt was already pitching great, I took personal offense when I got dropped as his partner, but only because I'd been living under my own veil of shame. From Matt's perspective the switch made total sense because he and Madison were *actually* playing in the playoffs and could feed off each other's adrenaline rush everyday. As for me, I was now a glorified batboy, albeit still getting paid more than Matt and everyone else. Even though I was hurt by his decision, I wasn't surprised. I would have done the same thing.

Being My Father's Son

A couple of years earlier, Dad had been diagnosed with congestive heart failure. But since he was generally distrustful of doctors his entire life, he never followed orders on how he should care for his condition. By now, he was eighty-two and I was thirty-two.

On Tuesday, October 12, just nine days after I had called Dad about quitting baseball, he started having trouble breathing. Eva, his caretaker, called Bonnie and told her she needed to drive up from San Diego immediately. She said that Dad was down on all fours struggling to breathe, but refused to allow her to call 911 or go to the hospital. Once Bonnie got there and convinced Dad to go, they raced to the ER. Seeing his condition, the doctors admitted him right away.

Within an hour, Dad's heart stopped. As he collapsed, a code blue was called and doctors and nurses rushed into the room to try and save him. After eight minutes with no pulse and multiple defibrillator attempts, my father was finally revived.

I was shocked to get the news about Dad because I wouldn't have been there to say goodbye if he had passed away. I couldn't help but think that his essentially dying in the hospital not long after our talk was more than a coincidence; that his will to live was somehow affected by the fact that I was close to giving up on the baseball dream—the dream that together *we* had worked toward for so many years.

Being that the Giants had already won our first playoff series and had a few off days before the next game, I headed to LA to visit Dad as he lay unconscious in ICU. With complete organ failure, doctors informed Bonnie, Sally, and me that he only had a 1 percent chance of survival. So here I was again, just like when Mom was in the hospital awaiting a liver transplant, trying to balance my baseball world with the pain of a parent dying in another city. But now, the two things I had placed my life focus upon—Dad and baseball— were *both* slipping away.

Since Amber and I had only been dating a few months, while I could never tell her at the time, she was my only source of stability at this point. I relied on her to give me the strength and hope I couldn't find anywhere else.

On one of my trips down, while Amber was sitting in the room, I went over to Dad as he lay there unconscious and began to whisper in his ear. "Hi Dad, it's me, Bear. I love you so much. And, hey, I had this idea about a trip we could take down to San Diego once you get out of this place. We could go visit every single field I ever played on and bask in those memories together."

I had no idea if Dad would ever wake up again. While I hoped that one day we could take such a trip, I was just trying to give him something, anything, to hold on to life. And I was grasping for any hope as hard as I could. I kissed him on the forehead and sat back down next to Amber. Without even saying a word, she comforted me, taking my hand and holding on so tightly as I let my emotions out.

As we sat in my father's hospital room, Amber's gentle presence made me feel like everything would be okay. In retrospect, I am glad I didn't tell her just how much of a necessity she was in my life, because I wouldn't have wanted to risk the pressure of driving her away. But I was so grateful to have her by my side through the entire journey.

Even with Dad incoherent throughout the playoff schedule against Atlanta and Philadelphia, I was flying back and forth between watching my team play and kneeling at Dad's bedside at the hospital. I didn't miss a single game, games that I had been told I didn't even have to show up for. But I *had* to be there. I *wanted* to be there. I couldn't stay at the hospital while my team played and I certainly couldn't just go back home. My work ethic, my team commitment, and my secret hope that I was going to be called on to pitch to redeem myself all fueled me to stay.

Managing the Madness

On one of my many trips back to LA, I left the airport and was on the way to the hospital. Knowing that my father could pass at any time, I sped past everyone on the highway. Suddenly, I saw a cop's blue lights flashing in my rearview mirror and then heard the siren. After we both pulled over, he walked up to my window and in normal protocol asked, "Do you know why I pulled you over?"

I answered, "Yes, I do. I was speeding, sir."

He responded, "Yes, you were. So where are you headed?"

In that moment, the dam holding back my emotions broke. "Well, my dad nearly died a few days ago and he's lying unconscious in ICU at Holy Cross. I just flew in from San Francisco because I'm a baseball player and we have a playoff game tonight, but I'm not actually allowed to play because I got taken off the roster. I had a terrible year but I still have to be there to support the team." I kept verbally vomiting and told this policeman way more than he wanted to hear. But it was his own fault because he asked me what I perceived at this point to be a very complicated life question, "*Where* are *you* headed?"

The most embarrassing part was that I started crying through all of my venting. Feeling really awkward now, he glanced at my license and said, "I thought I recognized this name—Barry Zito. The ballplayer?"

I stopped and said, "Uh, yeah."

He continued, "Man, I'm so sorry. That sounds like a lot. I tell you what—I'm going to just write you a warning. No ticket. I'll be right back."

That situation on the LA freeway proved just how fragile I was, on the verge of tears at any point and even looking to total strangers to help me with my problems.

In the spirit of full transparency, I have a dark confession to make. Through that painful playoff run, I began rooting *against* my own team. Yup, I said it. Hoping the Giants might lose best served my beat-down ego in two ways. First, I could finally get out of the Bay and go hide out in my home in Los Angeles. Second, if they lost, it proved they couldn't win without me.

As independent contractors, the downside is that when stripped to the core any player will fend for himself, even at the expense of his teammates. The reality is that even the best of friends on a team are competing for limited roster spots and in a way fighting it out to take care of their families. While that self-focused attitude may sound horrible and surprising to die-hard baseball fans, the reality is that I have had some baseball friends over the years confess to struggling with the same attitude. When challenged and isolated, our flawed humanness comes to the surface. In my situation, the selfishness overtook me once I felt like every Giants playoff win was bringing more embarrassment to my career.

During those twenty-nine gut-wrenching days of the historic 2010 Giants postseason run, I did everything I could to be invisible. I ducked concessioners while walking into the clubhouse before games. I tiptoed around the locker room to avoid getting in the way of my teammates who actually had to perform under pressure that day. I masked my shame with dark sunglasses and big headphones. Head down, music cranked, black Giants hoodie always over my head, with absolutely no eye contact with *anyone*.

As the team kept winning, playoff madness took over San Francisco. Even City Hall was lit up each night with the rally black and orange. Everyone was sporting Giants gear. Out of fear of being recognized and judged, I felt like I couldn't go anywhere. But I was so riddled with anxiety that I couldn't just hide out in my flat until it was time to go to the field. I often drove around for hours at a time listening to my favorite pianist and composer, Ryuichi Sakamoto. His instrumental projects naturally medicated me through my darkness each day.

Once Brian Wilson delivered the last pitch of the 2010 World Series, I knew I would soon be free to go home to start putting the pieces of my life back together. But now I had to make it through our championship celebration in the Rangers' visiting clubhouse. While people in San Francisco were streaming into the streets celebrating and going crazy, our locker room in Arlington, Texas, was getting covered in champagne.

I snuck behind the plastic sheeting and tucked myself as far back into my locker as I could to call Amber. She had, of course, been watching the game at home and was so excited. "Babe, can you believe it!? Congratulations! You won the World Series!" But I wasn't excited at all. I was numb. Amber's voice was the *only* lifeline I had left, so I kept her on the phone as long as I could. I didn't want to fake-celebrate with the guys. The sad fact was I don't think anyone even noticed my absence.

I probably should have been excited that my team won, but since I didn't contribute, I didn't feel like they were *my* team anymore. I felt unworthy to even wear my jersey, so I left it hanging in my locker and covered up in my black Giants sweatshirt. I wished I could have taken a plane straight to LA from Arlington, but there was one last thing to get through back in San Francisco. In each city, when its team wins a championship, there is a large parade thrown so all of the fans can come together to pay their respects to the players for cementing their city into sports history. Attending the parade was my final commitment to the Giants that year.

Being that we had brought home the first-ever title to San Francisco since the team's inception in 1958, there was a huge turnout for the parade, estimated at more than one million people along the one-and-a-half-mile route. Each one of us was assigned our own custom-decorated cable car. As I boarded my personalized trolley with the large print "Barry Zito" sign on the side, I made sure I again had on my large mirrored sunglasses to cover up the hurt. The car pulled away from the station on its way to City Hall and traveled at a snail's pace so the sea of fans could acknowledge each of us as we passed. As for me, I wished I could have kicked that trolley into fifth gear.

As I scanned the faces in the crowd through the falling confetti, I saw vulgar gestures directed my way, one after another—middle fingers coming from mostly the male fans but also from some women too. I could read the curse words on their lips. And on almost everyone, looks of total disgust. Waving and smiling as if none of the rejection bothered me, I began to feel like I was having an out-of-body experience. Trying to disassociate from my pain and shame for the hour-long ride brought me to the point of going totally numb.

As my last line of defense, I stopped making eye contact with people. Being on that cable car amid all the people that wanted me off the team and out of their city made me feel dead to the world and, even worse, dead to myself.

But throughout that horrible year, I never blamed anyone but myself. I never made an excuse, used anyone or anything else as a scapegoat. I took full responsibility for my failures and the consequences of my actions.

My poor performance was all on me. Realizing and owning that fact was the greatest pain of all.

11

But He Was Never There, Until Right Now

"I realized I'd been relying on my own strength for so long, and man, I'd been wearing it."

—My interview with ESPN[1]

Following the World Series, I went back to LA a broken man. Perched high in my mansion in the hills, the mountaintop view was as beautiful as ever, but I was seeing life through a dark, murky haze. Things couldn't get worse. Or so I thought.

Now, everyone wanted into Brian Wilson's world. My ex-roommate had become the man behind the "Fear the Beard" slogan that made him the most famous guy in sports in 2010, complete with talk show appearances and national TV commercials. He even took over my role as the famous ballplayer in the clubs. In all honesty, I resented him for hijacking my entourage along with the Hollywood fantasy that I had introduced him to just two years earlier.

Of course, Brian was just doing what any successful athlete in his position would do. Me included. My sense of feeling wronged by him and everyone else around me was so intense because I was looking at life through a clouded lens that told me everything was about me. The reality was that I had pushed Brian away and was totally to blame for my own unraveling.

I was living proof that a large bank account does not bring happiness or personal peace in life. In fact, having your salary posted on the Internet for everyone to see can create all kinds of hassles you could never imagine. The one and only stability I had left was Amber. But even with knowing how much she loved me, I still struggled with self-worth and sunk into a deep state of loneliness and depression.

Hi, My Name Is Barry Z

In my constant quest for answers and having now been humbled like never before, I called my sister Bonnie and asked her about something we'd discussed in the past—codependency. This disease stems from being so dependent on another person for your happiness that it becomes emotionally destructive to both people involved. The addiction is to a dysfunctional relationship, as in, "If you're not okay, then I'm not okay." A key component of codependency is low self-esteem that creates a search for *any outside source* to help a person feel better.[2] This described me perfectly and I was ready to get help.

After reading through the Codependency Anonymous (CoDA) website, I found the nearest meeting a few miles down the hill in the flats of West Hollywood. When I walked into my first CoDA twelve-step meeting and introduced myself, I quickly realized that nobody there had a clue who I was. That made me feel an immediate sense of safety. To keep things simple, I just told them I was an athlete. In hearing everyone's stories, I saw right away that—compared to me and my almost unlimited resources—these people had *real* problems. I don't mean to say I wasn't drowning in my own issues, but as humans who gain some wealth, we can all too quickly forget what struggling to pay rent feels like. That reality check was a positive element for me.

Much like Alcoholics and Narcotics Anonymous, CoDA also has twelve steps. Step one states: "We admitted we were powerless over others—that our lives had become unmanageable." Man, did I ever resonate with that one! Whether it was my father, the Giants fans, or the guy at the camera store, I had a laundry list of people I was powerless over and had let them all affect me in a negative way. Step two: "Came to believe that a power greater than ourselves could restore us to sanity." Um, yes please. Step three: "Made a decision to turn our will and lives over to the care of God as we understand God."[3] I could get with that.

Never afraid of homework to attempt a fix for problems, I dug into the CoDA manual and found the truths to be very powerful. I came to the sobering realization that there was an actual name for the insanity I had experienced for so many years: codependency. What I had done over the past decade was transfer the authority of my dad's influence over me onto my coaches, teammates, fans, and sports media. From one very close person to a million strangers.

I had become literally *obsessed* with other people's opinions of me, ranging from my performance on the mound to how many heads I could turn when I walked into a Hollywood club. But something was shifting in me because my past "positive mind-set" would have never acknowledged I was insufficient in *any* way. Now, by simply admitting that I was really messed up, the truth could begin to set me free.

Be Careful What You Pray

In early November, Amber did something in our relationship that I had never experienced before. I was at her apartment and we had just watched a pilot for a TV series for which she had gotten a role. The acting jobs were starting to happen for her. As I was lying quietly on the bed while she was reading a script, Amber began to cry. Surprised, I quickly asked what was wrong. She blurted out, "Bear, I can't do this anymore, this relationship. I need to be alone." I knew what it was like to have a girlfriend ask for space, but a full-on sudden breakup out of nowhere? No. I was in shock, totally dumbfounded. Devastated, I quickly grabbed my things and left. When I got in my car, I melted into a pool of tears.

This may sound strange, but I had actually prayed for years that someone would break my heart so I could know how that felt. I had certainly ended my share of relationships, and even though hurting those women that I cared for was difficult, I really had no idea how they had actually suffered. Well, as they say, be careful what you pray for, because God might actually give you what you ask.

For weeks, I was in and out of weeping. With my life in such shambles already, I watched the only good thing I had left tell me goodbye. During those difficult days, I wrote a song for her called "The Brightest One," with the last line being: "So go chase the stars, but never forget, you're the brightest one."

A few weeks later, after I returned home from Thanksgiving dinner at Sally's house, Amber texted me to talk. She said she had needed space only to get closure from her old relationship, and she now realized we were perfect for each other. With one text message, all the pain and confusion disappeared and my world was set right again. I had just been sobbing to my sister a few hours earlier, but now, as Amber was driving over to my house, I had tears of joy and gratitude.

Having kept all the lights dim in my home since the breakup, I went around to all the rooms and turned them up as bright as they could go. I then started playing Amber's favorite country music throughout the entire house. With the love of my life just minutes away, I fixed a quick candlelight dinner for us to enjoy when she arrived.

We got back together that night and have never been apart since. While I would never have admitted at the time that the breakup was good for me, those weeks apart proved beyond a shadow of a doubt how much I loved Amber and wanted to spend the rest of my life with her.

One of the things that always fascinated me about Amber was her spirituality. She would regularly ask me if I was okay with her praying out loud, and I would always say yes. I'd close my eyes and listen to her talk to her God like He was a friend that she had an actual personal relationship with. I was amazed at how she prayed so selflessly, always pouring out her heart in prayer for me and for my career. I had never done that for *anyone* unless they were very ill or close to death.

My entire life, I had always prayed to a force, not a person. My prayers were always about advancing my personal agenda. My only goal was to coerce some power out there to give me what I wanted. But Amber's prayers were always about what God wanted. She was raised a Catholic and her family has always been very committed to their church. But like so many young adults, she was confused by the hypocrisy she saw from people being in church on Sunday compared to their lives Monday through Saturday.

In spite of her apprehension about the church, Amber still felt a relational pull from Jesus and with her grandma by her side had asked Christ to come into her heart at the age of eleven. When her family wanted her to be confirmed in the Catholic Church at sixteen, she told them she wasn't ready to make a lifelong promise at such a young age. I respected the maturity in her decision, and that regardless of family pressures she had the courage to work out her own faith independently all those years.

Amber and I were obviously on the same spiritual journey, but coming from opposite sides of the spectrum. Leaving her hometown in Missouri at the age of twenty-one, she had started attending a church in LA called Oasis. That church had a powerful, positive impact on her life. She began to have a better understanding of what biblical Christianity was all about outside of traditional religious norms. Amber also started talking to me about a loving Father who had unconditional love and grace, and I wanted in on that, for sure.

As we were beginning a new year in January of 2011, Amber asked me to come to Oasis with her one Sunday morning. I was ready to go, always up for expanding my spiritual knowledge base. As the pastor started his sermon, he talked about trusting God with your money and giving to the church. Amber couldn't believe my first impression on her new spiritual home was going to be about asking for money. That's always a nightmare scenario when you invite someone to church for the first time. She assumed I would be offended and never want to come back. But my grandmother and mom had encouraged tithing at their church, so I understood the concept and had no issue with the message.

When we went back the next Sunday, the pastor challenged anyone sexually involved outside of marriage to stop and anyone living together that wasn't married to move out. Amber was frustrated again, thinking now I was surely offended and would never return. But always being teachable to new truths, I heard the heart of his message.

As the pastor was preaching, I leaned in to Amber and whispered, "I can do it. Can you?" She was shocked by my willingness to abide by the teaching. While we hadn't talked much about marriage yet, something was resonating inside me with these truths. In past relationships, I had experienced deep emptiness and unsatisfied longing as a result of premarital sex. In all those circumstances, the same story played out over and over. Someone always ended up with unmet emotional expectations. The difficult part was neither of us could communicate correctly to the other because to some extent we were always "playing the game," trying to never fully show vulnerability in fear of losing the person.

Sex always complicated the relationship and tainted the honesty of the interaction, always with one giving sex to get emotional security and the other offering emotional security to get sex. Without sex involved, there would have been so much less pain. Sharing your body with another person has become so matter-of-fact and commonplace today that everyone seems to ignore the emotional emptiness that results from the physical interaction. In my opinion, the physical will *always* affect the emotional.

So from my personal experience and response to this teaching, I wanted to fully feel my love for Amber without shutting off those parts of me. Hearing clear-cut lines of morality in her church that day made perfect sense to me. I was ready to commit to trying these beliefs connected to the Bible. And I felt like there was something much deeper behind all this new thought.

Desperate Measures

Dad had been in the hospital for about three months, incoherent but hanging in there far beyond the doctor's expectations. From his heart stopping for so long, his feet began slowly turning blue, with one getting worse than the other. When they put a stethoscope on them, they couldn't hear a pulse. The blue slowly gave way to completely black, while the skin on his feet began to look like plastic.

The doctor told Bonnie, Sally, and me that, while Dad still being alive was a miracle, to prevent systemic infection they needed to amputate one of his legs above the knee. Making that decision was so difficult for the three of us because all his life Dad had been hypercritical of doctors, saying, "All they want to do is cut on you!"

So here we were with Dad unconscious, making the decision to allow a doctor to "cut on him" and take away his ability to walk, should he recover. In his will, Dad made his wishes abundantly clear that he wanted every measure taken to keep him alive, so ultimately his own directives helped us know what to do. We all agreed to the amputation. While the first surgery was successful, within a month they had to take his other leg too.

A few weeks later, Dad miraculously regained consciousness. That very first conversation we had was so interesting. After he opened his eyes and acknowledged us all, I grabbed his hand and asked, "Hey Dad. How are you feeling?"

He looked so content, with this warm expression on his face like we'd never seen before, responding, "I am just fine, Barry. It's so nice to see you all here in my room. I love you all very much."

We were so nervous to break the news to him about his legs but knew he deserved to know. Sally began, "Dad, we want to tell you some things that happened while you were unconscious. Infection was spreading through your body and so to save your life the doctors had to amputate your legs just above the knee. It was such a difficult decision to make for you, Dad, but we felt you would have made the same one to survive." She paused to let her words sink in a moment and then gently asked, "Are you okay, Dad?"

The crazy thing was he didn't even react. It was like he didn't care that he'd never walk again. He just smiled that warm smile of his and repeated, "Barry, Sally, Bonnie, I'm so glad you are here. I sure do love you guys."

What was happening? This was not the same guy who had the heart attack months earlier. Something was different.

A few weeks later, to everyone's surprise, the doctors determined that Dad was healthy enough to go home. The only ongoing issue was, after the initial heart attack, his kidney function never came back, so he had to have regular dialysis.

Having lost his hair in his early thirties, Dad always wore a hairpiece and was ashamed of his bald head. But at eighty-two years old, he often told us, "I'm really just a bald old man." He seemed to accept himself authentically as he was and never wore that hairpiece again.

Dad's new grateful and appreciative disposition was such a drastic change from the guy who constantly drove me toward fame, success, and wealth all my life. His heart softened in a way none of us could have predicted. He rarely asked me about baseball after that, and when he did, he only wanted to know if I was happy playing the game. Many times he had me recount childhood memories of when he and I practiced baseball together. As I recalled the past, he lay there quietly, listening intently, gazing up at the ceiling with a heartfelt smile across his face. I felt for the first time I was seeing the man my father truly was, behind all the bravado of having to prove his worth to the world. There was nothing more beautiful than experiencing his pure heart.

He became less concerned about *what* I was doing and more concerned with *how* I was doing. Dad often asked whether Amber and I enjoyed being in love. Amber had met him only once before his heart stopped, so her view of him was much different than mine. She only saw this gentle soul that had a childlike love and appreciation for us all, following his near-death experience.

A Rose Among Thorns

As the dreaded 2011 season began, I was the fifth starter and was only in the rotation because I was making $18.5 million that year. Of course, from the front office to the coaching staff to my teammates, everyone was hoping something, *anything*, might help me become the pitcher I was getting paid to be.

My first start that season was against the Dodgers. Because we were going to be coming from San Francisco into LA, I arranged for a rental car at the airport so I could drive home and sleep in my own bed. On the way to the house, heading east on Sunset Boulevard, I went to take the left onto Sunset Plaza just like I'd done a thousand times over the past ten years. As I turned into the intersection, a taxi driver gunned his car to beat the red light and T-boned me at forty miles per hour. My car spun around like a top from the impact.

Once the car came to a complete stop, I remember being in a daze, seeing the shocked looks on the people's faces who were eating at Café Med across the street. When reality set in, I realized my neck was hurting badly. After being taken to the hospital by ambulance, the ER doctors didn't find any breaks and released me in a few hours.

Implementing my do-whatever-it-takes work ethic, I got on the phone and flew in my chiropractor and massage therapist from San Francisco. Knowing the accident was going to cause me to be very sore the next few days, I did everything possible to regain my mobility and flexibility. For two days, I had to wear a neck brace. But by Sunday for my start, I was able to play and actually threw the ball surprisingly well.

Two days before my third start versus Arizona, we had a day off that landed perfectly on Amber's birthday. Since the team schedule was released months prior, I had been formulating the ideal plan to whisk Amber off to Napa Valley and ask her to marry me on the day she turned twenty-five. I made sure I wasn't pitching the day following our off day so I could stay in the Bay while the team flew to Phoenix. I approached Bochy for his blessing, and after hearing my plans, he graciously agreed.

I prearranged a private tour at Napa's highly coveted Harlan winery. Amber and I drove up from San Francisco and arrived by late morning. Even though her birthday was enough reason to leave the team and take her away, I also knew she was going to be sniffing out a possible engagement. I had to be extra prepared to maintain the element of surprise. Toasting with champagne overlooking Napa Valley would have been a great time to propose but was also way too obvious.

We went to another nearby winery on a private tour of their wine caves where they stored all their barrels for aging. We then headed to Calistoga for lunch, where I attempted to further divert Amber. After appetizers, I dropped down on one knee for a couple of seconds only to go into a hip flexor stretch that I commonly did on the field to combat tightness in my lower back. She was not at all happy with that move and laughed nervously when I sat back down at the table. While probably a crude thing to do, I thought it'd be a good way to throw her off my trail. I had been growing a mustache for the past month, which also worked in my favor. She later told me, "I never thought you would propose to me with that thing on your face."

The last stop of the day was the famous Jordan winery. The employees there were Giants fans and graciously allowed us to stay in a special private guest room that wasn't normally open to the public. After we put our bags in the room, I staged a phone call by texting the hospitality department to ring us on the landline while Amber was freshening up in the bathroom.

Speaking in a loud voice, I answered the phone. "Hello? Oh hi, yes, we just got here. Oh wow, that's so nice." I paused in key spots to allow for the fake conversation. After all, I had done a little acting too. "So you guys want to meet us for some wine down on the balcony by the oak trees? That'd be great. We'll be right down." I told Amber I had to meet some of the Jordan staff under the trees just outside the room and that she should walk down when she was done getting ready. She agreed and didn't suspect a thing!

I headed down and made sure the CD player was hidden in the

bushes and that the disc I had sent by FedEx a week prior was cued up on my favorite song, "What Are You Doing the Rest of Your Life?" by Stacey Kent. Amber soon came down the stairs, sat at the bistro table under the trees, and began marveling at the views. I hit the remote to start the song as I began opening a bottle of Jordan cabernet. I handed it to her, asking that she remove the cork. From there, everything seemed to go in slow motion. As she took out the cork, she noticed some bright red writing on it that read, "Amber, will you marry me?"

At that moment, with the song playing in the background, I dropped to one knee, took out the ring, and waited for her to respond.

"Yes! Yes, I will!" she exclaimed.

A photographer I hired had been secretly taking long-range photos and now came in for some close-ups. With the moment just as magical as I had planned, the best part was (Amber told me later) that she gave up on the hope of getting engaged that day when I had faked her out at the restaurant. My plan worked! She and I will never forget our special day that began the journey of the rest of our lives together.

I joined back up with the team for my game in Phoenix. In the second inning the pitcher came up to bat. After I threw my pitch, I saw him square around to bunt. As I bolted to the plate, I felt a strong pop in the arch of my right foot. Incredible pain shot through my lower leg. The doctors diagnosed the injury as a "lisfranc," where the ligament that holds the foot bones together is traumatized and at times even torn.

Fortunately, the MRI showed the ligament was not completely torn. That injury could have ended my career. But the ligament was sprained, or more accurately, stretched. The doctor put me on crutches to keep the weight off my foot with the prognosis being a healing time of two to three months.

Coming to the Crossroads

Since entering the big leagues eleven years earlier, I had never missed a start due to injury but now I was at home watching my team play on TV. With time on my hands, I was back on the hunt for a new answer. Lying in bed with my foot propped up, I had at least five books open all around me.

Knowing the depths of my personal pain and depression, Amber had been praying about how to help and what she could say to me. When she walked in that day to visit, she saw me surrounded with books and trying to read them all at once. She calmly stated, "Barry, I need to talk to you." I looked up from the pages and nodded. She continued, "Babe, I think you need to lock all your books up." Now she really had my attention. Surprised, I asked, "What? What do you mean?" With grace in her voice, Amber explained, "Yeah, lock them all up, and I want you to start reading just one book."

She handed me a Bible and said, "*This* book."

That was one of the most powerful moments in my life.

Out of love for me, Amber took a stand. She was serious and very sincere, so I listened intently as she added a challenge that led me to the biggest crossroads of my life. "Barry, do you think God is trying to tell you something? Look at what has been happening: you're left out of the playoffs and World Series, the car accident, and now this strange injury to your foot. You might want to pray about what is going on here."

The very interesting part about her and God's timing was that for the past couple of weeks I had started attending the team's Tuesday afternoon Bible studies. The chaplain was Jeff Iorg. There were only a few of us players there each week. I was so desperate and so hungry that I had been taking in every word Jeff taught. After the other guys left, I stayed to ask him questions about Christianity and the Scriptures. I wanted to know about Jesus and the Christian

God that I heard Amber pray to. I wanted to understand how He was different from the force I had prayed to all my life.

Sensing Amber was right, I did what she asked. I put the other books away and started to read the Bible. I also kept going to Jeff's Bible studies. He was in the book of Ephesians and, one day, he read chapter 2, verses 8 and 9, which say: "For it is by grace you have been saved, through faith—and this is not from yourselves, it is the gift of God—not by works, so that no one can boast."

Grace . . . through faith . . . gift of God . . . not by works . . . so that no one can boast. A single sentence wrecked my spiritual paradigm. I had always heard about grace but never understood. The idea of anything being given that I didn't need to *earn* and *couldn't take credit for* was life changing to me. For so long, I had been relying on my own strength to save myself—from myself. Sounds like a walking contradiction!

I had encountered so many people who were raised "in the box" in some form of Christianity and were desperately trying to get out. But being raised "outside the box" like I was, I craved solid structure in my spiritual life. I began to view the Bible as my instruction for life. *Sin*, *hell*, and *evil* were always bad words in my home, because just saying them could "give life to negative things." If we ever said something Mom believed to be negative, she quickly responded with, "Cancel, cancel." So learning the actual meaning of the spiritual words was eye-opening.

Realizing that there was a real enemy trying to sabotage my mind and heart every day was mind-blowing, but made total sense! Having been an "all is love" type of person, I could never quite understand why the world was so screwed up, me included, if there was no actual force of darkness. As I listened to Jeff teach the Bible, I felt I had discovered something I had been denying the existence of my entire life. And the idea that "this world is not my home" resonated instantly.

My grandmother Ann's promo picture for singing gigs.

Joe Zito and Nat King Cole doing their thing in the studio.

Nat in the middle; Mom on the right.

Here's my mom: Roberta Zito.

Mom & Dad's wedding, 1964.

Barry William
2 weeks, 1 day
May 28, 1975

SPRING CHICKEN!
ME TAKING IN THE WORLD AT JUST TWO WEEKS OLD.

DAD LOVING ON ME.

MY SISTER
SALLY AND ME.

HERE I AM AT THIRTEEN YEARS OLD.
PRE-BRACES, OBVIOUSLY.

SAN DIEGO IN 1992.
MOM, DAD, MY SISTER SALLY, AND ME.

MOM WORKING HARD AS A PASTOR.

AT THE U.S. OLYMPIC FESTIVAL IN COLORADO SPRINGS, COLORADO, IN 1995. BONNIE, ME, SALLY, AND MOM.

LOOKING SHARP FOR SENIOR PROM.

MY HIGH SCHOOL GRADUATION IN 1996.

MY SOPHOMORE YEAR IN JUNIOR COLLEGE. MOM WAS JAUNDICED HERE, PRE-LIVER TRANSPLANT.

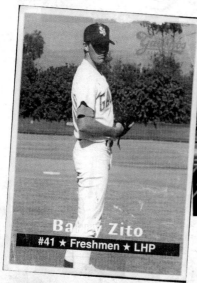

Barry Zito
#41 ★ Freshmen ★ LHP

PITCHING FOR THE OAKLAND ATHLETICS IN 2002.
HERE, WAITING OUT A RAIN DELAY IN PITTSBURGH.

MY FIRST
BASEBALL CARD!
PITCHER FOR UC
SANTA BARBARA.

THE BIG THREE:
MYSELF, MARK MULDER,
AND TIM HUDSON.
THIS WAS THE
MINNESOTA TWINS
LOCKER ROOM IN 2002.

ON THE OAKLAND A'S TEAM PLANE.
ME SHOWING OFF MY LATEST THRIFT STORE PICKUP,
WITH ERIC CHAVEZ IN THE FOREGROUND.

THE WHOLE FAMILY AT MY AWARD DINNER FOR THE CY YOUNG IN 2002.

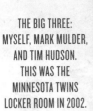

SPRING TRAINING OF 2004. JAMMING WITH LEGENDARY BASEBALL WRITER PETER GAMMONS.

DAD MINUTES BEFORE MEETING ONE OF
HIS HEROES: GEORGE W. BUSH.

DINNER AT THE WHITE HOUSE IN 2004.
ENJOYING MY CONVERSATION WITH FIRST LADY LAURA BUSH.

HANGING WITH ONE OF THE
GREATEST BANDS OF ALL TIME.

MY LOCKER MATE IN 2007, PREPARING TO BREAK SOME RECORDS.

My Infinite Mind is Superior to Circumstance

ONE OF MY SPIRITUAL AFFIRMATION POSTERS.

MY SETUP FOR SPIRITUAL/MENTAL TRAINING IN A MINNEAPOLIS HOTEL ROOM.

MEDITATION ON CAMELBACK MOUNTAIN IN PHOENIX, ARIZONA.

MY HOUSE IN HOLLYWOOD HILLS, CIRCA 2006.

MOM AND DAD ENJOYING THE VIEW FROM MY PLACE IN MARIN COUNTY, CALIFORNIA.

DAD AND HIS SISTER ROSE,
WHO WAS MUSSOLINI'S GODDAUGHTER.

MOM AND DAD ALWAYS SUPPORTED MY BASEBALL CAREER. ALWAYS.

THIS WAS ME JUST MINUTES
AFTER THE GIANTS WON THE
NATIONAL LEAGUE WEST IN 2010.
SMILING THROUGH THE PAIN.

THE MOST MAGICAL DAY OF MY LIFE!

ME AND A NEWLY PREGNANT AMBER
IN SAN DIEGO.

DAD AND ME IN HIS LIVING ROOM.
I'M HONORED TO BE PART OF HIS LEGACY.

BUSTER POSEY, MYSELF, AND BAM BAM MEULENS
THIRTY MINUTES AFTER WINNING THE 2012 WORLD SERIES.

RECEIVING MY 2012 WORLD SERIES RING
IN FRONT OF THE HOME CROWD.

THROUGH MY LENS—THE 2012
WORLD SERIES PARADE.

THE ZITO FAMILY!
TAKEN IN NASHVILLE, 2018.

Running Home

My ankle healed and was strong again, so I was activated in June. With a fresh start, my first three games back were amazing as I won them all, posting a 1.29 ERA. But the next three games went downhill again at three innings with eight runs, seven innings with six runs, and five innings with five runs. Still in the playoff hunt, Bochy had to make another tough call. Once again, he was forced to pull me from the rotation. He knew he couldn't send me down to Triple-A because of my service time, but yet he couldn't trust me to pitch either.

Since I had no experience pitching in relief and couldn't help the team in the bullpen, Bochy went with his only viable option of putting me on the "Phantom DL." This is kind of a no-man's-land in pro baseball. DL, of course, stands for disabled list for injured players. But this imaginary zone is a team's last resort when they need a roster spot for a new player, but can't get rid of the inferior player. The only way around this is to make like the struggling guy is hurt, putting him on the DL. But internally, everyone knows that player is not actually hurt at all. To make it jive with the media, I just told them, "Yeah, my right foot started giving me problems again."

Being told the plan, and understanding the circumstance I had put the team in, I complied. Putting a player on the DL means a spot can be opened up on the twenty-five-man roster for a new player. But once September comes, there's no need for the DL because forty players can be on the major league roster. At that time, the minimum stay on the DL was fifteen days, so I knew I was going to be invisible in the clubhouse for at least that long, while working hard to solve my pitching woes.

During those two weeks of being a phantom, on August 9 we were playing Pittsburgh at home, and I arranged to meet Jeff early at the Tuesday Bible study to talk more about Jesus. Just as the times before, all his answers made perfect sense to me. After he answered

my last question, he carefully offered, "Well, Barry, we can pray a salvation prayer right now if you want." I was *so* ready. After all the weeks of Jeff patiently answering my many questions, giving me the space to process and come to my own decision, here we were.

I affirmed, "I'm in. Let's do it." Jeff began to pray and I repeated after him. But after a bit, I began to take off on my own, inspired by Amber's prayers I had always been so fascinated with. I remember so well saying the words, "Jesus, I believe You are my Lord and Savior. I want to live for You now and not for myself anymore."

As soon as our prayer ended, I was flooded with all kinds of emotions and feelings. After the many years of my doing all I could to find something real, now Someone had come to me and taken over my life. Not just spiritually and emotionally but also physically and mentally, I felt that happen. There was a change in me that was as real as the breath in my lungs.

I hugged Jeff and thanked him for his patience and help. He encouraged me to read a chapter in Proverbs every night with Amber. When I got home, I told her the news that I had finally found something that was *real*. She expressed how proud she was of me that I had been working things out on my own for months, just like she had been doing in her life. But we both knew the crossroads came when she challenged me and presented me with the Bible. Amber was eager to jump into Proverbs together to strengthen our faith.

I knew my spiritual life was now vastly different because my faith in Christ had nothing to do with pitching. I sensed this new relationship I had entered into wasn't about to be proved or disproved by the results of a game. I didn't have to worry if this truth was going to sustain me over time or fall apart quickly like every other one before. The resonation was throughout my entire being, in *all* my life, not just on the mound where all of my spiritual focus had been placed before. I was so relieved to be all in on a structured set of beliefs, something that was unchanging, unlike the constantly mutating,

emotionally driven worldviews of my past. No more searching. No more Barnes & Noble trips for the latest self-help book.

I knew I had arrived at the last stop on the journey.

I *knew* that I had found the answer for *my* life.

The war was over and I could begin healing.

I was home.

Experiencing Grace

Six days later, on August 15, Bochy called me into his office and told me that since I hadn't pitched in two weeks I needed to get some work in with the Triple-A team. Since standard procedure is to play at the lower levels before coming off the DL, I agreed to go down and make some "rehab appearances," knowing full well my body was fine.

On that first start in Fresno, I gave up a ground ball to first base, and as I sprinted to cover, I tripped over myself, severely spraining my right ankle. I fell to the ground screaming in pain. I went from "fake hurt" to badly hurt. No phantom this time. Now I had to rehab several weeks for real.

I worked hard to get healthy and returned to the team on September 16. I pitched an inning each in four games. In the last week of the season, I went in for what I knew to be my final inning of the year. As I retired the first few Colorado hitters, something happened that to this day I do not understand. The fans started chanting my name. "Zito! Zito! Zito!" Somehow, and now I could say it with sincerity, by the grace of God, some of them were *still* with me. The only thing I could figure was that seeing how I had hung in there all that time, and always being a professional through it all, had produced a sympathetic response in Giants fans. Regardless of the reason, that was such a touching and meaningful moment for me.

Once the off-season arrived, Amber and I started putting the final touches on our wedding plans at the Marin home. We put a deck over the pool and transformed the backyard into a magical venue. Dad was healthy enough to be there, so we flew him in on a private jet to accommodate his needs. The ceremony was beautiful, with about one hundred people attending. One of the greatest moments of my life was watching Amber walk down the aisle to the same song I played for her at our engagement: "What Are You Doing the Rest of Your Life?" Our marriage began in the same backyard where we shared our very first weekend together eighteen months earlier.

After all my years of scouring the universe for answers and in the face of all the horrible days of my baseball career in 2010 and 2011, I finally found real salvation and redemption in life through Jesus. My life was *changed*. I met my Best Friend and Lord on August 9 and married my best friend and soul mate on December 3.

THE REBIRTH OF BARRY AND AMBER

My name is Pastor Jeff Iorg and I am the president of Gateway Seminary. In 2011, I was the baseball chaplain for the San Francisco Giants. I was at the ballpark on Sunday, August 7, when Barry came up and asked if I was going to be leading Bible study as usual on Tuesday. After I told him yes, he asked, "Could you possibly come early? I'd like to ask you some questions."

Now, players often asked to meet with me, only to not show up. So my trust was low. Our Bible study was at 2:00, so we agreed to meet at 1:00. Barry's last words were, "Thanks, I'll see you there." But I was doubtful.

Tuesday came and I brought some work with me in case Barry didn't show. I walked into the locker room at 1:00, very surprised to see him waiting on me. Gracious as always, he said,

"Hey, thanks so much for coming, Jeff."

Sitting down in the meeting room, he got straight to his questions. "What does it mean to be born again and have your sins forgiven?"

I answered, "Those two things are very closely connected. Having your sins forgiven is a part of being born again." Barry's questions kept coming, and I did my best to give biblical responses.

Seeing how he was taking in the truth of Christ after our spiritual back-and-forth, I finally said, "Barry, I have just one question for you. Are you willing to commit today to invite Jesus Christ into your life to be your Savior and Lord?"

With conviction and certainty, he answered, "Yes, I am."

I continued, "Great, then we need to pray."

Barry smiled and agreed, "I'm ready."

I started the prayer and Barry followed my lead. But after several sentences, he took off and began pouring his heart out to God in such a beautiful way. What happened next will be forever etched into my memory. After we finished, Barry leaned back in his chair, looked me in the eye, and confessed, "All my life people told me that I could find God if I just looked deep enough within myself. But He was never there—until right now." In that moment, I knew something powerful and very real had occurred in Barry's heart. God, through Christ, had found him in his wandering and brought him home.

Over the next few weeks, I began helping Barry see how he could align his life to the Word of God. In one of those early meetings with him and Amber, we talked about marriage, how faith intersects with a Christian couple, and their upcoming wedding. After the conversation concluded, they began to look at each other the way couples often do when they are trying to send nonverbal signals.

Finally, Barry said, "Well, Jeff, we have an issue. We had asked my meditation coach to marry us, but because I'm a Christian now, I want you to do the ceremony." Amber agreed. Later, when Barry spoke to his friend, he ended up having to cancel so everything worked out well for us all.

In the weeks ahead, Barry called one day and asked if I might visit with Amber privately. I gladly agreed. Since my very first meeting with Amber, I knew she was a God-fearing woman who had a heart to love the Lord. She told me about asking Christ into her life when she was eleven at her grandmother's church. But now as an adult, she wanted to commit to Christ anew—renew her vows, so to speak—fully aware of her decision for the rest of her life. After talking through her spiritual journey, I had the privilege of praying with Amber to secure her relationship with Jesus, just as I had prayed with Barry.

One year later, I received a card in the mail from Amber. Her handwritten message said, "Pastor Jeff, thank you for your help in my journey of faith with Christ. This past year has been amazing. My life has been changed. I am growing and learning so much and just wanted to say thank you."

When we have the opportunity to present the gospel to someone, if they choose to invite Christ into their lives, we are simply like a midwife. We only assist in the birth of the new life, having nothing to do with conception or creation.

One of the great highlights of my ministry are those two moments when I had the privilege of leading Barry to faith in Christ and praying with Amber to seal her decision for Jesus once and for all. And I will never, ever forget Barry's powerful confession to me: "All my life people told me that I could find God if I just looked deep enough within myself. But He was never there—until right now."

Stay on Your Side of the Fence

"The entire experience was about God. It was not about me."

—My interview with CBN[1]

Baby, I can't take this anymore, the pressure, the expectations, the abuse. I'm sick of being Barry 'The Worst Contract in Baseball' Zito. I wanna go home."

As we sat on the front porch of our Arcadia, Arizona, rental house a week into 2012 spring training, I confessed to Amber what I didn't have the strength to say to myself.

She responded, "Barry, I'll always support your decisions, but I know God has a purpose for all this, and you need to trust that He will see you through this entire seven-year contract. Don't give up, Baby. As God sees this, everything is happening perfectly."

Little did I know at the time how prophetic her words actually were.

Stirring in the depths of my misery that spring, I handled adversity quite differently this time around. Every time before when I got to my emotional breaking point, I stopped believing whatever teaching I was following at the time. I wanted to move quickly onto something new that might inspire me in a fresh way. But now, not for a second did

I doubt that Jesus was the answer. In fact, the opposite was happening—I knew *I* was the problem, *not* the teaching. Unchanging, Jesus was perfect and so was His message. I was the one with changing to do, but I couldn't do it myself. The only way was to lean further into Him and get in God's Word daily. I devoured the book of Job to remind me how to be faithful in times of deep question and struggle.

In accepting my own insufficiency, I opened up to His proficiency. I still marvel at the fact that as the deep spiritual seeker I was for so many years, I never ran to another spiritual doctrine after discovering the God of the Bible. That alone was evidence for me that Jesus really was the truth.

Just a few days later, as I was sitting alone outside by the pool, I began to pray about my baseball career. I did what so many Christians do when confused about God's will. I said, "God, if I'm supposed to stay in this game, show me a sign that will alleviate my doubts."

Soon after whispering that prayer, a hummingbird came out of nowhere and buzzed my face with that unmistakable sound of its supersonic wings. Throughout my entire childhood playing ball with Dad in the backyard, there was a hummingbird that was always back there while I was practicing. When I realized what happened after my prayer, I looked up to see the little bird hovering near a palm tree by the pool, almost as if he were saying, "Want me to dive-bomb him again, Lord?"

A strong sense of peace came over me that echoed Amber's words to not give up. God had brought me this far and wasn't going to abandon me now. I recommitted to baseball that day and decided to do all I could to silence my will and walk by faith, trusting only in God's will for me.

Prayers in the Closet

As the season progressed, I stayed in God's Word and my spiritual growth was helping me see life more clearly than ever. Jesus' teaching was ringing true: "But seek first his kingdom and his right-eousness, and all these things will be given to you as well" (Matt. 6:33). For the first time ever during a season, I removed the false idol of baseball from the altar and put God where He had always belonged.

Each morning I expressed gratitude to Him that I was even able to wake up that day. Entitlement had left the building and I was walking in full appreciation of the fact that I got to play a kid's game against real major league players in the most beautiful stadiums in the world. With God's will as my first priority each day, I focused simply on honoring His gift by doing the best I could with what He had given me. I submitted my life to Him *daily*. I valued His peace over wins and losses. Of course I was still competitive and wanted to win, but I was more concerned with God's will being done. When anyone told me that I played a good game, I no longer felt it was *my* game. My response became: "I'm just out there throwing the ball the best I can. God's got the rest."

In the first game of the year, I pitched a rare shutout at hitter-friendly Coors Field in Colorado. With 2012 being my best year as a Giant, I won fifteen games, lost eight, and posted a 4.15 ERA. The team won my last eleven starts, and as a result of our efforts, we made the playoffs.

The day before our first postseason game, Bochy called me into his office for a very different conversation than the many others we had before big games. "Z, you got game four in Cincinnati." I lit up like a kid and thanked him. I then ran into a nearby closet, fell to my knees, and thanked God for the opportunity I knew He had given me. After five turbulent seasons with the Giants, I was finally going to pitch a playoff game! After performing well in multiple postseasons for the A's, I was excited to get to pitch in the postsea-son as a Giant. I was committed to going out there focused on the process, not on results.

In that first round of the playoffs against the Reds, we lost the first two games in San Francisco. So we had to win the next three back in Cincinnati to advance. We headed east and won game three, which meant I would be pitching an elimination game the next day.

But my humanness took over and the Enemy started whispering in my ear. The old feelings of insecurity and inadequacy were like sharks circling. My mind-set reverted back to proving to Giants fans that Zito could deliver when they needed him most. No surprise that my game ended up a disaster. Bochy pulled me out in the third inning. I couldn't believe I had allowed my ego to sabotage me again. Tim Lincecum came in and dominated, leading us to come back and win.

Staying at the Westin Hotel in Cincinnati, Amber and I had gone out for ice cream that night. I was *not* doing well. Staring blankly at the walls, I confessed to her how numb I felt after spoiling my one chance to make up for all those crappy years as a Giant. She reminded me that we could still advance to the next round. But I knew even if we did pull off a win the next day, I was certain I had lost the coaches' trust to perform again.

But once again, Amber was right. We shocked the baseball world and won game five in Cincy. We were the first National League team to climb out of a 2–0 deficit in the Division Series. In the second round, a best of seven series, we hosted St. Louis. Madison Bumgarner, who was normally dominant, had a tough day and we lost game one. After winning game two, we flew to St. Louis for the next three games.

Once in Busch Stadium, Lincecum and I were at neighboring lockers for the off-day workout when pitching coach Dave Righetti came in and said, "We are giving Bumgarner a break this time around, so Timmy, you got game four and Zito, you got game five." Once again, I ran to a private room around the corner, dropped to my knees, and thanked God for yet another opportunity to glorify

Him. I prayed, "This time, Lord, I won't sabotage my gift. This game is all Yours, God, whatever You want it to be."

We lost the next two games, so my start became an elimination game just like in Cincinnati. If we lost, our season was over. That morning at the Westin, I turned my cell phone off and unplugged the hotel phone. I wanted *no* distractions. I didn't want to hear any sports news or see what people were saying on social media. Amber and I kept the conversation light and listened to music like we always loved to do. I'm glad I made the decision to stay off the grid because "#RallyZito" was trending big on Twitter that entire day. The fan movement was equally flattering and encouraging, but I am so grateful none of that was able to get in my head.

Following his pregame rally speech, team leader Hunter Pence asked if I wanted to add anything. Never being one for speeches, I shared, "Look, boys, I can handle losing today, but I won't be able to sleep this off-season if we go out there and give *anything* less than our best. Our best is *all* we can do anyway, so let's go enjoy this."

As I went through my pregame routine, I had one focus: "Stay on your side of the fence, Barry." Honoring God was more important to me than winning the game. I knew He wanted me to trust my pitching abilities and not worry about the results I couldn't control. I was committed to just being Barry and let God be God. My priorities were so aligned that I also told Him, "If you want me to give up ten runs, I'm cool with that." Not being about me anymore, I felt total freedom out on the mound. The game felt like slow motion, because I was so in the moment, so engaged in giving my all on each pitch. I *knew* I was not alone out there.

I didn't care who got on base or what the situation was, because I wasn't working for the Giants that night. I was working for God and honoring His gifts in me. The old Barry would have crumbled, but the Holy Spirit directed my every move, keeping me totally calm in a sea of playoff craziness. I even had the presence of mind to successfully lay down a surprise bunt with two outs. I got the runner in and knocked the Cards' starter out of the game with the momentum-shifting blow. That play was later referred to as "the bunt heard around the world" by Giants fans. I went on to pitch almost eight innings and we won the game 5–0.

That game was the best of my entire career, but I couldn't take credit for the win. God deserved the glory. But others, of course, tried to glorify me. The folks in the media were all personally excited for me as they brought their barrage of questions. But all I could say was, "I was blessed to throw the ball as well as I did tonight."

After we stunned the Cardinals, the series went back to San Francisco and we rode the momentum to beat them two more straight, securing a spot in the World Series. The next day was a workout off day in our home park as we prepared to host the Detroit Tigers.

Bochy and Righetti called me into the coach's office. Speaking through a huge smile, Bochy said, "Well, Z, looks like you're pitching game one of the World Series." I could tell he really enjoyed giving me the news, knowing what we had been through together. All the three of us could do was laugh. And right after that, as you may have already guessed—I ran to the closet to thank God.

Express, Not Impress

I waited until I got home to tell Amber in person. Like two kids who were just told they were going to Disney World, we started jumping around the room, hooting, hollering, and praising God. The game was twenty-four hours away, but I was already so full of joy just to receive the once-in-a-lifetime opportunity to pitch in the World Series. And in front of my home crowd, no less! I knew God had brought me this far and the results were all His now. Miraculously,

I had *no* stress. What would have felt like pressure and fear for the old me was now only childlike excitement. My "yoke was easy and my burden was light."

On the day of game one, the parking lot was full of TV trucks for the international broadcast. When I sensed the old triggers of fear and expectation, I responded each time with total gratitude and reminded myself that I didn't get here alone and wasn't alone today either. I had come full circle from "Be the Man" to "God's the Man." I was only there to express His gifts, no longer attempting to control the universe.

I called the new mind-set my "bubble of control," meaning once the ball left my hand, I had done all I could do and the rest was up to God. I knew I wasn't responsible for the actions of the hitters, the umpire, or the fans. Throughout the day, I utilized a breathing exercise where I took only six breaths per minute. Slow body, slow mind. No more frantic out-of-control thoughts. I was living life in real time, in the moment.

I was starting against Justin Verlander, who had won the Most Valuable Player *and* the Cy Young the season before. The MVP is a hitter's award and the Cy Young is, of course, a pitcher's award. Rarely does a pitcher win both, but Justin was literally dominating baseball. Before the game, I was lying on the training table, watching the sports commentators on TV. They were all talking about how Justin had only given up a couple of runs in his last seven games and how he was going to crush us that night too. Seeing how the odds appeared to be stacked against me, my reaction was peculiar: I just laughed.

I took the mound at AT&T Park that evening with the world watching. I pulled my hat down, focused on my breathing, and fixated on the catcher's glove. I repeated to myself: "My *only* job is to throw the ball the very best I can, and God will take care of the rest."

I got into a few jams early in the game, but being so calm out there helped me to never spiral into my fear of failing. I gave everything I had to every pitch. My defense made some spectacular plays behind me, and at the plate Pablo Sandoval stunned Verlander by taking him deep in each of his first two at-bats. I got in on the action, too, coming up to the plate in the fourth inning with a runner on third base and squaring up Verlander's 97 mph fastball for a base hit to left field. With that hit, I became the fifth Giants pitcher to knock in a run in as many playoff games, which broke a major league record.

I pitched almost six innings and gave up just one run. Lincecum came in after me to finish. Dethroning the top pitcher in baseball was a whirlwind as we won 8–3.

After the game in front of all the media, they were firing questions like, "Barry, do you feel redemption now from 2010?" I answered, "I don't know about all that. I'm just grateful that I threw my pitches the way I did." The irony about redemption being everyone's focus is that I tried desperately to redeem myself to the city of San Francisco for many years and never could. And now that I had the redemption, I didn't even want it. I had something better, the Redeemer Himself.

We ended up sweeping the Tigers in four games, two at home and the final two in Detroit. I didn't try to *impress* anyone, but only worked to *express* what God gave me. For so many years, I tried so hard to *take* from the game of baseball through approval, fame, or redemption. But now I had *given* my all to the game with no expectations of getting anything in return. What was returned to me was the greatest thing I could have ever wanted—a World Series Championship. The feeling of being so immensely blessed in that moment was completely different from my earlier efforts of creating my own reality. I knew this was not about me at all but all about Him.

The last pitch of the World Series was a fastball from Sergio Romo taken by Miguel Cabrera for strike three. We rushed the mound and went crazy on the field. Back in the clubhouse, champagne was exploding and madness ensuing. Just as the coveted World Series trophy was brought in, a media person pulled me into the hallway for an interview.

When I finished and walked back into the locker room, the entire team, including Bochy, was huddled in a circle, holding up the trophy, and chanting, "Barry! Barry! Barry!" I just looked on, speechless, flooded with emotions and the memory from two years before when I was hiding from the celebration. My team was showing me so much love from everything I had been through the last six years, honoring the fact that I fought my way back.

Two days after our big win, the city threw their second World Series celebration in three years. But this parade was the polar opposite of two years before for me. The cursing and middle fingers had been replaced with chants of "Zito! Zito! Zito!" As soon as my parade car came into view, people started screaming praises. I felt the love as deeply as I had felt the hatred two years before. The ride ended with all of us gathering for the official presentation and speeches in front of City Hall.

As the off-season began, I was sitting out on the back deck of the LA house by the firepit on a beautiful fall night, journaling to God. That season, Philippians 2:13 had become a theme verse for me: "For it is God who works in you to will and to act in order to fulfill his good purpose." He placed the desires in me and then gave me the power to fulfill His purpose. Pitching was no longer from me and for me, but from Him and for Him. I was no longer confident in myself but in Him. I had learned the hard way that fulfillment in life is not found in accolades and contracts but in the daily pursuit of abiding by the "still, small voice" of God inside that aligns me with His will. Experiencing success without shouldering the weight of all the credit and instead giving it to Him was such a liberating paradigm shift.

The Eighth Year Option

Going into 2013 spring training, I had one season left. My contract was seven years with an option for eight at $20 million for that year. Coming off the World Series and still being very healthy at thirty-four years old, I wanted to play as long as I could. Taking on Dad's lofty goals, I hoped to get in twenty years of service. But there is a strong temptation in the final year of your contract to prove you are worth getting picked up for that additional option year. Those old familiar feelings of having to win people over began to stir again.

Scott, my agent, told me, "If you go out and dominate the league, they *might* pick up your $20 million option, but in all reality with your age, they probably won't. So play this year out and we'll get you a one-year deal next year where you can go win a spot in the rotation." Hearing his words of advice confused me. I had just helped my team win the World Series and then, only a year later, it was considered "fortunate" to even get a spot somewhere? Old fears crept in. I digressed spiritually to the concept of "my will" again, instead of submitting to God's.

During our first home stand in San Francisco, the World Series ring ceremony was held on the field. Back in 2010 I got booed when I came out to get my ring, but for this ceremony, they were standing and cheering.

I was on fire to start the season and won my first two games. Going back to the end of the 2012 season, the team had now won my last seventeen starts. Then we headed to Milwaukee, a hitter's park where I had always struggled. I stumbled and gave up nine runs in two innings but then pitched well the next game. Up and down with my performance, by mid-May I was 6–5 with an ERA over 4.

Feeling desperate for results like in days of old, I fell back into a fear-based performance mind-set. I even dabbled with some of the new age teachings I had used in years past. But one day in the struggle, I realized, just as Paul talked about in Romans, that my flesh was battling my spirit. I believed I was being tested to see if my behaviors were matching my belief that I couldn't do life without God. So I made the choice to step back and submit to His will again. I was beginning to understand that repentance was not only a one-time event but also an ongoing process.

Dealing with the possibility of not getting picked up by the Giants for another year and being uncertain of what the next year looked like, I started contemplating retirement. While Dad and I never talked about baseball anymore in his new state of health, I wanted to call him to talk over my thoughts.

Remember the first time I had called him about quitting baseball?

Another Gift of Grace

When Dad got on the phone, he said, "Oh, Barry, my son, it's so good to hear your voice."

I began, "Hey, Dad, as you know I'm in the final year of my Giants contract, and I want to know how you feel about me retiring after this season?"

Dad answered, "Well, Barry, you have worked hard to make a good life, and you have a wonderful marriage, too, so if that's what you really want, then do it." *Who are you and what have you done with Joe Zito?* I was shocked by his response. But with Dad's blessing I felt the freedom to finally make a decision for myself whenever I was ready.

Soon after that conversation, I came home from the field one night and this odd sensation came over me that my mom was speaking to me. Or somehow the Holy Spirit was relaying a message. I felt like she was saying that Dad was only staying alive because he thought I needed him. I had to release him. Over the next several hours, I couldn't shake the feeling.

The next day, I called and delivered the message, "Hey, Dad, you know I don't need you to stay around for me anymore, right? You have given me so many tools in life, and with Amber and my financial stability, I'll be more than okay. If you need to go, then do what you have to do, all right?"

Dad responded, "Oh, Barry, that's nice. Thank you so much."

Three weeks later on June 19, 2013, Dad quietly passed.

A few months before he died, I made some calls to try and find a pastor who might go visit him to offer some spiritual comfort. Jeff, the Giants chaplain who led me to Christ, helped me find Pastor Eddie Pate. I called and he graciously agreed to visit Dad. Eddie began to go see him once a week and talk to my father about the Lord. In preparing for the funeral with Pastor Eddie, he told me that, just a few weeks before his death, Dad had prayed with him and given his life to Jesus.

Taking into account the wild spiritual journey that my parents and I had been on for so many years, knowing that both my parents had come to faith in Christ in their final days was miraculous. And I was so grateful to God.

After Dad died, I let go of everyone he had hired to take care of me: the publicist, accountant, and attorney. I cleaned house and took full control over my career, my finances, and my life. At thirty-five years old, I was starting all over, on my terms, as my own man.

Finding Favor

Following Dad's death, I returned to the team and three days later threw a gem of a game at home. But that was not the norm that summer. By the end of July, I was taken out of the rotation. Bochy sent me to the bullpen. I was just grateful to not be put on the Phantom DL again. We clearly weren't going to make the playoffs, so that allowed me to stay around.

The strange thing through that summer of struggles was that I was doing all the right things on the mound. But the results weren't good. My entire career, if I gave up runs, the reason was because my pitches weren't coming out of my hand correctly. But this time they were. I was executing on my end but still giving up too many runs. Something was going on and I prayed my spiritual ears would be open to listen.

One day while shagging balls in the outfield, I kept sensing that I was being told to take a year off from playing baseball. Not to retire, but step back and work on pitching by myself for a while, just like I had done as a kid. The crazy idea rose up inside, and I knew I had to listen.

I called Amber from the road and told her. Her first response was, "Don't get my hopes up, Bear! After this crazy life we've lived with you being gone so much, the thought of us being together for a year is awesome. But are you sure?"

In LA on a road trip, when my agent, Scott, came out to the field, I threw my idea at him. He responded, "I think that's the worst thing you can do, Barry. You can't just take a year off at thirty-five. The game will be too fast when you come back. Just play this year out and we'll find you a new deal for next year." But I wasn't convinced. I was deferring to the Holy Spirit now, not anyone else.

The entire second half of the season, I was in the bullpen. Then during our last home stand, Bumgarner's elbow flared up. Righetti came to me in the clubhouse and asked if I could start the next day, which was a rare request on such late notice. I knew that game was likely my last start as a Giant. I pitched five innings and gave up one run to get the win and beat our rival Dodgers at home.

A day later, the *San Francisco Chronicle* released an article reflecting on the last seven years of "the Zito contract." Hesitantly, I made my way through each line and read something that I never expected to see in print. Brian Sabean, the guy who signed me, said,

"As crazy as this sounds, it might to you folks, if I had to do it over again, I would have done what we did to sign Barry Zito."[2] I couldn't believe what I was reading. For fans to say something about me was one thing, but when a statement like that was released internally, it meant something totally different. I felt so vindicated to read that the Giants didn't regret the decision to sign me as much as I was convinced they did.

Before the last game of the year, Bochy called me into his office and asked if I wanted to pitch one last time as a Giant. Completely fired up, I said yes. Late in the game, he told me to get ready to pitch the eighth inning to face just one hitter, the Padres' Mark Kotsay, a former teammate of mine from Oakland.

As I jogged to the bullpen to warm up, the crowd saw me and started cheering. I took the mound against Kotsay and struck him out. The fans went crazy. Ironically, that was his last at-bat in his career. Thinking I may have just thrown my last pitch in the big leagues, walking off, I smiled and tipped my hat to the fans as they continued standing and applauding.

As I came into the dugout, Pablo Sandoval grabbed me and pushed me back out onto the field, encouraging me to soak in my final standing ovation in San Francisco. As I stood there, waving and looking around the stadium, 40,000 fans began chanting, "Zito! Zito! Zito!" Every player came out onto the field and hugged me. Amber was there in the stands, living that surreal moment with me. Seven very long years were officially over.

Later back at home, I turned on some music and sat down on the bed by Amber. I was overwhelmed with the experience at the field and began to cry. And then she began to cry too. For thirty minutes, we lay on the bed, weeping together.

I think I released all seven years of pent-up emotions in that one evening.

No Regrets, No What-Ifs

"My baseball career has been a mirror to my life off
the field, full of euphoric highs and devastating lows."
—My interview in *MLB News*[1]

God was probably having a good fatherly laugh over Amber and me. Deciding our plans were to settle down for good in San Diego, we bought the "last house we'll ever live in," to quote our exact words. The home was ten minutes from the best waves in San Diego, so I was in for life. We jumped into a major remodel, expected to take at least a year. As the off-season and my year off began, we sold both the Marin and the Hollywood Hills homes, leaving San Francisco and LA for good.

Waiting on the San Diego home to be done, we rented a house on the beach in the Bird Rock neighborhood. Having plenty of time on my hands now, I went surfing every morning. I got better than I had ever been before, even tackling ten-foot waves on a trip to Maui. Each day after surfing, I set up my portable pitching mound and practiced in the backyard overlooking the Pacific Ocean. Just like Dad and I had done years earlier, I set up a video camera and analyzed my form. Sometimes I took my net and a bucket of balls to the park to throw for hours.

In November of 2013, we found out Amber was pregnant with Mars, our first son. We were super excited about having a baby. By taking off the year, I was going to be home through the entire pregnancy and for sure be at the hospital for his birth. Because of road trips, so many ballplayers can't get there in time when their children are born.

When spring training time rolled around, it felt so good to not have to go back to the grind but just stay committed to my daily regimen of weight training and pitching practice by myself. I was also reading Scripture and growing in my faith. The time away offered me the space and opportunity to see who I was in Christ—without baseball. You can't really know how much of your identity is wrapped up in something until that thing is no longer in your life.

Aside from the spiritual benefits of taking a year off, I felt myself connecting with the game in a way I never could have if I were trying to win in front of thousands of people. The quiet space that was created allowed me to fall back in love with the simple act of throwing a baseball. With the exception of a few stints along the way, I had been pitching from a place of fear for too many years. I was now getting back to pitching from a place of love, like I did when I was a boy. Regardless of whether I would make it back into the major leagues or even pro baseball, I was getting exactly what I had hoped by taking a year off.

Mars was born July 6, 2014, and Amber and I began the adjustment of being new parents. After we got him home and settled in, I traveled to Montgomery, Texas, outside of Houston, to train for a few days at Ron Wolforth's Baseball Ranch. Seeing that Ron's pitching program was effective for me, I called Amber and told her I loved the experience there. I wanted to come back for a few days every six weeks. But being the incredible support my wife has always been, she insisted that we just move there to capitalize on training for my final four-month push to get back into pro baseball. After we prayed to be certain that was actually God's plan, we packed up the house in a week and moved to Houston. Once there, I started a deeper level of preparation for my 2015 season.

If You Say You're Ready, You're Ready

A few weeks before spring training began I talked to Scott, my agent, and he started calling teams to see who might be interested in me. Different organizations sent their scouts to come watch me throw bullpens at a local field. Just like my early days, they brought their radar guns to measure my velocity. The entire time, I just kept praying for God's will to be done.

As I mentioned before, velocity is such a big deal to teams. But when not in a game and adrenaline hasn't kicked in, maximum pitching speed is hard to reach. Before the coaches and GMs started coming to watch that winter, I was only hitting 81 mph. Surprised at how slow I was throwing, I got defeated and started dissecting my motives and intentions for trying to play again. When I was a boy I pitched because I loved nothing more than throwing a baseball. Then once all the attention and fame was thrust on me, I began to pitch to please everyone. Throughout my career I toggled between the two, like an inner tug-of-war.

Once I saw the digital readout on that radar gun barely get me into the low eighties, I questioned whether I was really doing this for the love of baseball. Or did I just want to show the baseball world that Barry Zito would come back stronger than before? Was I trying to prove anything? Did I want something for myself outside of God's will? But after praying, I felt confirmation that this crazy plan to leave the game and come back was the Holy Spirit's, not mine.

Within a week, I threw for the Royals, Indians, and Rangers. My trainer heard from the scout that I was hitting 87 to 88 mph, which was a huge relief. The Houston Astros' owner and manager came out to watch and afterward asked me to come to Minute Maid Park to throw a bullpen. They wanted to utilize their "TrackMan," a device that analyzes pitch rotation far better than the human eye.

A week before spring training was to begin, I was getting ready to go pitch for Houston when I felt I needed to text Scott: "What about Billy Beane and the A's? Can you see if he's interested?" Billy had always told me he would love to have me back with Oakland one day. Scott agreed. An hour later, he contacted me to reach out to Billy.

The A's had just signed with their new Triple-A affiliate, the Nashville Sounds, complete with a brand-new ballpark that was being built near downtown. Of course, I loved music and had always been intrigued by Music City. Ironically the past several years, I had an art piece hung in the music room in my Hollywood home of Nashville's city skyline. My goal was to make the big-league squad, but if I had to go to Triple-A, playing in a songwriters' town was the ideal scenario.

Billy and I always had a great relationship. In fact, I never saw him the way he was depicted in the movie *Moneyball*. I called him the next day and he told me, "Z, we would love to have you here. I'll bring you in to spring training, but you'll likely start the season down in Nashville."

Surprised, I asked, "But don't you want to see me throw to make sure I'm ready?"

He laughed and said, "Z, you know I trust you. If you tell me you're ready, then you're ready. With your work ethic, I'd never question you." So I signed with the A's for the second time in my career.

Remember when I talked about players signing with the teams who brought them up? Gratefully, my credibility with Billy from seven years prior was still intact.

After four months of living in Houston, Amber, Mars, and I

headed back to major league spring training. I didn't have social media at that time, but a friend of mine had posted that I was coming back to Oakland. My phone started blowing up from everyone calling and texting me. We rented a house in Arcadia, Arizona, again, the same area we had lived two years before. But I didn't feel much anxiety about having to go pitch, only a childlike appreciation for the chance to play pro ball again.

In spring training, I easily shifted back into the morning baseball routines I had become accustomed to for fifteen years. The big difference was this time my faith had created a sense of gratitude that I had never felt before just to be in uniform. I was back in the big leagues and felt I had heard God correctly to take a year off and come back. The big surprise that I didn't see coming was the other players were viewing me like an Oakland A's legend. There was even a huge poster of me from the Cy Young year hanging in one of the clubhouse hallways. Ironically, I felt like a rookie again, with this wide-eyed sense of awe as if I had never been in the big leagues before. While at the same time I was being looked up to in the locker room by all the players.

In the first game, I pitched against the Cubs and hit 89 mph. The media summary was: "Zito is looking good." I threw the ball well that spring but couldn't compete with the big-time A's prospects that had major arms, all throwing in the mid-90s. Scott had been right about the game being faster when I returned. At the end of spring training, they called me in and said I wasn't going to make the team. They gave me the option to leave to pursue another club or go down to Nashville. My excitement for baseball was no longer affected by my status in the game. I was just eager to enjoy baseball again, just like I did as a kid in the backyard with Dad, even if it was in Triple-A.

The media swarmed my locker, intrigued with the fact that an established veteran was going to accept a minor league assignment. I answered their questions with, "I am just grateful to be pitching again, and I've actually always wanted to go to Nashville." I meant every word.

At the time of my decision and the team's announcement, we were playing a preseason series in Oakland. I was staying at that same Airport Hilton where I spent my first night as an A years before. I called Amber and said, "Honey, we're moving to Nashville." She responded, "Baby, what!? Are you okay?" Always holding my dreams in her heart, she was convinced I was going to make the big league team. I continued, "Yeah! We're gonna love it there. Nashville's a great town and way closer to your family in Missouri."

Old Dog, New Tricks

We found a new sense of adventure in moving to Music City. But I had to get reacquainted with the Triple-A lifestyle again: 5:30 a.m. flights and three-star hotels, landing and going straight to the field to play. I was back in the baseball grind in a big way. My first few games were rough as I adjusted. After pitching poorly, there were a few times I was tempted to walk into the coach's office and retire.

After one especially bad game, I called Amber and said, "I've had my fill. I'm good now. I'm going to go in and tell the coach I'm done and come on home." Every time she heard me out and then said, as only a patient, loving wife can, "No, Barry, you can't go out like that. You have to see this through and hang in there to see what God has for you." Deep down, Amber wanted me to be home with her and Mars, but she knew there was a bigger picture. God wanted me to see baseball through to the end and walk away only when *He* said I was done.

A's veteran Ben Zobrist had come to the Sounds on rehab and led a Bible study for the team. We were studying Romans and camped out in chapter 8, verses 5 and 7, where Paul says, "Those who live according to the flesh have their minds set on what the flesh desires; but those who live in accordance with the Spirit have their minds set on what the Spirit desires. . . . The mind governed by the flesh is hostile to God; it does not submit to God's law, nor can it do so."

Those words resonated in my spirit, so to recommit to being led only by *the* Spirit I had to loosen my grip on baseball, which for so many years had been a desire of my flesh. Feeling more freedom than ever, I started having the time of my life on the mound. I pitched twenty-six straight scoreless innings. There were whispers that I should be called up to the big leagues again because I was pitching better than some of their guys. But now I was encountering the forty-man ceiling. Someone had to come off the roster for me to be called up.

After my injury-plagued season in 2011, I had recorded an album of four original songs that I had registered with ASCAP, an organization that receives and distributes publishing income for songwriters. Then the first summer I was in Nashville, the *Tennessean* newspaper released an article and interview with me where I talked about wanting to write songs.

After the article came out, Robert Filhart, at the time the creative director at ASCAP, emailed me to talk and send him my songs. After he had listened to them, he called back and asked, "Are you a Stevie Wonder fan?"

Surprised by the question, I answered, "Yeah, he's one of my biggest influences. How could you tell?"

Robert answered, "Even though your song 'Home' sounds country, I could just tell there was some Stevie in there. So, I love your songs and would like to set up some cowrites for you with some writers in town."

I was blown away at the opportunity and told him I still had a summer of baseball to play before I could commit to anything else. Robert began sending me songs from other writers to listen to and learn from. I also ordered every book I could find on Amazon about songwriting and the music industry. Between my games I read music books in my locker for hours, and the guys always joked about my newfound discipline.

Having not thrown in a game the year before, I began to feel arm pain for the first time in my career as I approached 130 innings that summer. But I just pushed through the pain because I knew this was my last season.

After my run of scoreless innings, God had made it clear to me that I had received what I came back for—enjoying the game like I did when I started my baseball journey thirty years earlier. In having my stretch of successful games over that summer, I was reminded one last time that baseball could never fill me up the way I hoped for most of my life. While I certainly enjoyed that hot streak, I didn't attach my identity to my performance. That gave me a sense of freedom I never felt before. I could finally say for certain that I was just a man who loved to play baseball and nothing more. Not a superhero, not God's gift to the human race, just a man. Pitching that year in Nashville gave me a new sense of humility and appreciation for everything I'd experienced on the field as a professional. I knew I was ready for my next step in life.

The last Sounds game of the year was in Omaha. After the game, Ryan Roberts, a good friend who was also a veteran who had significant big league time, came up to me as we were all walking back to the clubhouse and said, "Hey Z, put this blindfold on." Then the guys began chanting my name, popped some corks, and proceeded to douse me in ice-cold champagne. Once I entered the clubhouse, I heard the music blaring. Removing the blindfold, I saw pictures of me covering the walls. Amber was on the road trip and had all my favorite desserts delivered. The guys threw me an incredible surprise retirement party. It felt so weird to suddenly be done with the game that I had been playing almost every day for three decades.

In September 2015 I was officially finished with baseball and back home for good in Nashville. Robert started setting up a calendar for me of cowriting sessions with songwriters. I was excited about launching into my new career in music. I had put a nice period on the end of the baseball story and was ready to begin writing a new chapter in music. But after only my second songwriting session, on the drive home, my cell phone rang. The name that popped up on my screen was Billy Beane.

One More Last Chance

I answered, "Beaner, what's up?"

He said, "Hey Z, you got any bullets left in you?" *Surely he didn't mean what it sounded like?* "Billy, you know I'm retired, right? Just played my last game a week and a half ago."

He continued, "Well, we've had a couple of guys go down with injuries and we could use a little help up here."

My first thought was no. In fact, I got a bit angry inside, thinking, *Why couldn't you have called me two weeks ago, before I retired and powered down all the breakers on my baseball career? Was I just some emergency plan?* I hadn't touched a baseball in nine days, which is an eternity for a pitcher during the season.

Billy explained, "It's September, so we have more roster spots now. We're hosting the Giants in our park in ten days, and Tim Hudson is slated to pitch. With his retiring this year, too, we all think it would be super cool for the fans if we squared you guys up in the Bay." Blindsided by his offer, I told him I needed twenty-four hours to answer.

Having accepted a week earlier that I would never again play pro baseball, I went home in a daze of confusion and told Amber. "You are never going to believe this, but Oakland wants to call me up to pitch the last three weeks of their season."

Amber was stunned but excited. A huge smile came across her face as she said, "Baby, that's amazing!"

I was *not* smiling and went on, "I don't want to go. I finally have closure with the game now. I don't feel the need to go redeem *anything*. I am done."

Amber, surprised at my attitude, stated, "What?! But Babe, you have a chance to pitch in the big leagues one last time."

That night I went back and forth many times about the decision, but finally we decided I would never have another chance like this again and that my songwriting could wait until I got back home in a month. There was really no risk. My contract was still in play with the A's, so all I had to do was say yes.

The next morning I contacted the team and told them I was in. They put me on a flight to meet them in Chicago, having not played there since 2006. Walking into the White Sox visiting locker room, I felt oddly out of place, like I didn't deserve to be there. I explained to all my teammates about Billy calling and their plan for me to pitch against Huddy. They were all very gracious to me.

After flying to Houston, on my third day back with the team, they put me in for an inning. Out on the mound, I felt like a fish out of water. I had never felt so foreign out there and so overmatched against the hitters. Even just a month before, I was equipped and ready for the opportunity, but since I turned off my baseball brain in every way, trying to reengage was so difficult. Under the circumstances I held my own but still gave up a two-run homer.

Next, we returned to Oakland to face the Rangers. Every pitcher out there was throwing 95 mph. Once again, Scott's words were ringing true—the game was getting too fast, and I felt I couldn't keep up.

The night before the big Zito-Hudson face-off in the Bay, Tim and I met in the press conference room to do a side-by-side interview for the media. We had a great time playing up our battle and giggled through the whole thing.

Ever since I could remember I wore high socks like the old timers, making me feel like a real baseball player. Even in the recent era of "cool" players wearing big baggy pants that cuff around their shoes, I never changed my look. So that day on the field in Oakland, every player on the A's pulled their socks up high to honor the Zito aesthetic. I felt so flattered by their gesture of respect toward me.

Pitching on the mound of my youth as an Oakland A again was nostalgic to say the least. Then seeing all my old Giants teammates step in the box made things even weirder. But *all* the fans, both Oakland and San Francisco, were cheering for me. They even sold collector's posters of Huddy and me that said "Aces Forever." Even though the fans had fun with the reunion, neither Tim nor I pitched well, and I was upset how my magical moment had gone terribly wrong.

Following that game, I considered letting the team know the next morning that I was going to pack up and head back to Tennessee. But when I told Amber my plan, she stated, "Oh no. You need to see this through. You need to finish out the final week with the team, like you promised." Accounting for her track record on pep talks, I knew she was right and agreed.

That next day, when I had planned on possibly telling manager Bob Melvin I was done, he walked up and asked me if I could throw on two days' rest and make one final start in Anaheim versus the Angels. I was elated to get one last chance, especially since the Angels were playoff contenders and I would get to face their full-strength lineup. With the excitement of a kid, I immediately called Amber and told her the news, to which she jokingly replied, "Wow, Barry, well I guess you won't be quitting today then, huh?" Yet again, she was proved right.

Everyone I knew came down to that last game in Anaheim. What an amazing day. My final performance was a start in the big leagues. On the mound, I pitched four innings and gave up two runs. And we won! In this final season after God had told me to take a year off and come back, He had orchestrated every last detail as I closed out a major chapter of my life walking with Him. With that final season in the sport I had committed myself to for all those years, God gave me the opportunity to leave the game with no regrets. I was liberated from the what-ifs in regard to my career in baseball and could move forward into the next arena of my life with a sense of closure. This is something few get to experience in the game, and I feel was yet another undeserved favor of grace from God.

A Beautiful Mystery

If you had told me back when I was a rookie that I would fall short of my and Dad's baseball goals of twenty years played with three hundred wins, I would have deemed my baseball career a complete failure. And I would have been sure to wear a veil of shame the rest of my life for not making the Hall of Fame. That may sound a little absurd because I did have a pretty good career, but it only proves that, living according to the flesh, there is a void inside of us that cannot be filled any other way than through Christ.

Being blessed to stay healthy, to pitch for fifteen years, and to win a Cy Young and a couple of World Series didn't matter to my flesh, because it was only concerned with getting more and more while never being satisfied. But now, in being led by the Spirit, my new worldview allowed me to see my career in a way I never could have predicted, with total gratitude and a sense of awe.

In this culture of striving for personal achievement, I know not taking credit for my baseball career sounds strange. Sure, I worked hard and was disciplined, but anyone can commit to those concepts. I don't know why my body never broke down and I stayed healthy, or why I had a special curveball, or how I helped save the Giants' season in my St. Louis game in 2012. But I can't take credit for any of those things. My life is really a mystery to me.

Ever since that day with the Giants chaplain in 2011, I stopped living Barry Zito's story and began living God's story. That's the beauty of giving my life to Christ. I live for Him now. Even though I didn't realize it until I was thirty-three years old, He was and is the Creator and now gets all the credit for anything good in my life.

Once covered in shame, I now embrace my crooked path in life, because every twist and turn was a part of His story for me. If I did have ten Cy Youngs in my closet and three hundred wins in baseball, I would still be searching for my identity somewhere on the streets of Hollywood.

One of the biggest blessings that came with my relationship with God was my ability to embrace every flaw and mistake from my past. They brought me to the sacred place of total humility that opened the door so Jesus could walk into my life.

He is my Redeemer.

I am at peace with my journey.

I wouldn't change a thing.

Conclusion: The Tale of Two Rings

> "We can rejoice, too, when we run into problems and trials, for we know that they help us develop endurance. And endurance develops strength of character, and character strengthens our confident hope of salvation."
>
> —Romans 5:3–4, NLT

Having been a part of the 2010 and 2012 championship Giants teams, I own two World Series rings. Even at the height of my ego, I never wanted to be "that guy" who flaunted his rings out in public. In fact, I *never* wore them. Tucked away in my closet for years, those rings never left their cases. But in 2017 an invitation came that changed my mind.

Two years after retiring from baseball, I received a call that I was going to be inducted into the National Italian American Sports Hall of Fame in Chicago. Connecting my heritage from Dad's side of the family with my fifteen-year baseball career was such an incredible honor.

As I began to plan my speech, God placed something specific on my heart. I told Amber, "I think this induction will be the first time I wear my rings out of the house. If I don't wear them for this, I probably never will." She was surprised because of how I had always felt about them but was relieved because she never understood why I hid them.

At the event up on the podium, I held up my two rings, one in each hand, and said, "Here's my 2012 World Series ring. In this run, I was deemed the Giants savior in the NLCS and five days later won game one of the World Series. I definitely earned this one. But here's my 2010 World Series ring. I didn't do *anything* to deserve this one. I wasn't good enough to make the playoff roster, so out of self-hatred and insecurity I rooted against my own team, hoping they would lose without me. When I walked out onto the field to receive this ring, the entire stadium booed me. This has always reminded me of my greatest failure and for many years I despised this 2010 ring.

"You might think the ring I would be most proud of is my 2012 ring. But that's not the case. It's the 2010 ring. Why? Because that ring was much more difficult to earn. Watching my team, game by game, achieve the one thing I wanted more than anything in life, to win a World Series, was the most difficult situation I have endured in my life. Especially because I got signed for a ton of money four years prior to lead them there.

"Having placed my full identity into my baseball career for most of my life, only to have it stripped away during the 2010 World Series run is what led me to discover my *true* identity. Not in a game, but in Jesus Christ. In 2011, I surrendered my life to Him and after that, any achievements were not my own, but His, including this 2012 ring.

"After stepping back from the intensity and pressure of being in baseball, I see things more clearly now and realize I must embrace my greatest failures, for they are the ones that made me who I am: wiser, stronger, and more equipped for this turbulent ride of life— all through Christ. These two rings may look alike, but in my eyes they are worlds apart. So I'm asking you, what do *you* value most and why?"

To this day, I still have people come up and talk to me about the 2010 season. One dad told me, "My son is a young baseball player. As he and I watched the 2010 playoffs and World Series, we noticed how you dealt with adversity. I was able to use you as an example and tell him, 'How Zito is handling all that is how you should walk through difficult times with integrity, Son.' We'll never forget the way you handled 2010."

For fans to express appreciation for how I dealt with that experience means so much now. It took everything in me that postseason to stay with the team, to stand up to the media interrogations, to always be kind to fans, even when they weren't kind to me. I had to make a conscious choice to *not* run and allow the failure to scar the rest of my life. Only then was I able to experience the victory on the other side.

The interesting and ironic thing is, while I felt such incredible *shame* in 2010, I didn't have its twin brother *fear* in my heart. My dad always told me, "A man is only as good as his word." I made a commitment to the Giants that for seven years, come hell or high water, I was going to show up no matter what. No choice. No hiding. No running, even though everything in me wanted to flee. But my work ethic and integrity were always the most important things in my life.

I *had* to keep my word. I had signed a contract promising to show up and play, or at least be ready to play if called upon, so my only fear was not holding up my end of the deal. I had to swallow my pride and be a professional. For whatever reason, I could never do what was easy. No matter what, I was going to do the hard thing. Going home and hiding just felt cowardly to me.

After fifteen years of being able to live my dream of playing pro baseball, I arrived at the realization that I would much rather hear comments about my *character* in 2010 than *compliments* about my performance in 2012. Hearing how I inspired someone to endure and keep going another day in tough circumstances means far more to me than how well I pitched in a game. While this may have taken me years to learn, I believe character matters far more than performance in the long run, and certainly matters more to our Heavenly Father.

God's Gift of Mercer

After having our son Mars, Amber and I experienced several miscarriages over the next couple of years. As anyone knows who has walked through one, the event is heartbreaking and often traumatic. And the more you have, the more hopeless you feel. But Amber and I continued to pray for God's provision of another child in our family.

In Nashville, we had become friends with Chad and Teryn, another married couple. In 2013, Teryn had been on a reality TV show called *Preachers' Daughters* with her dad, a pastor, and her mom, Victoria, the head of a pregnancy resource center. As Amber had gotten to know Victoria through Teryn, she had a strong sense that God was going to have Victoria somehow bring us a baby. Of course, these centers are not adoption agencies, so we knew that couldn't be the vehicle God would use. Nevertheless, Amber felt so strongly that she began to call Victoria her "stork," while also having specific visions about the child.

One night in February of 2017, Victoria texted Amber with only these words: "Call me."

Amber felt right away that the text had something to do with a baby. She called Victoria immediately, and through her tears, asked, "You have my baby, don't you? And he's African American, isn't he?"

Victoria began to cry, too, and answered, "Yes, I do, Amber! And he is African American!"

Overhearing the conversation, I didn't know what to think. Amber and I had never committed to adoption because we were hopeful she would birth our next child. I actually got upset and began pacing the floor, mistakenly thinking she had somehow planned an adoption without me. But of course, that wasn't true. Amber was hearing *all* this for the *first* time too.

Victoria began telling Amber the entire story of a twenty-one-year-old woman who had been a victim of sexual assault. The girl had seen Victoria on *Preachers' Daughters* and was so inspired spiritually that she had given her life to Christ. Feeling strongly connected to Victoria now several years later, the young lady had reached out to her on Facebook to seek guidance after the sexual assault had occurred and her pregnancy was confirmed.

This being such a traumatic experience, the woman considered abortion twice after finding out she was pregnant. But each time she felt the Holy Spirit urging her to keep the child. She had been raised in foster homes and already had two children, so she didn't want to place him into the system. Multiple adoptive families fell through and the woman was at her wit's end trying to find a home for the baby inside her.

The mom-to-be said she felt like God told her Victoria knew the couple that would be this baby's parents. Of course, Victoria immediately thought of Amber and me. The due date for our last pregnancy that miscarried had been May 6, 2017. The young woman told Victoria the baby's due date was May 6. Yet another clear sign of God at work.

Amber was all in, but I had just heard everything for the first time and needed to get with God to pray about everything. I called a good friend who adopted their child and found out that he had been adopted too. I told God all of my fears and expressed my worries about taking a new family member into our home in just three months' time. But within twenty-four hours of hearing the news, I felt a strong confirmation from the Lord that this baby was *ours*.

About six weeks before the due date, we rented a home near the young lady in Georgia, and she graciously allowed us to go to all her final prenatal appointments. We began to help her financially as well as walk through all the legalities to officially adopt the baby. During the time there, Amber had received another strong spiritual warning that there were going to be problems at the birth, possibly even a threat to the health of the mother.

Finally, we got the call that she was in labor and headed to the hospital. When we arrived, the nurses broke the birth mother's water to speed things along. A nurse who was also a Christian told us she sensed the Lord tell her to place a monitor on the birth mother's belly, even though that was not standard procedure. And thank God she did because within minutes, the monitor showed that the baby's heart rate had dropped from 140 to 70. Doctors and nurses flooded the room and rushed the birth mother into surgery for an emergency C-section.

Helpless, kneeling in the hospital hallway, Amber and I immediately began to pray at a depth we rarely had before. Finally over the sound of our prayers, we heard a baby's cries coming from the operating room. We soon found out that he had a prolapsed cord, and once they took him out, he had coded on the table and nearly died. They revived him, and he went straight into NICU, staying there for a week until the doctors released him. His birth mom was fine. Amber's vision of chaos in the delivery room was accurate, but thank God, everyone ended up in perfect health.

On May 14, 2017, Mercer Joseph Zito was born, his middle name to honor my dad. Two weeks later, we took him to his new forever home in Nashville with his big brother, Mars. We have also stayed in touch with his birth mom, sending pictures and updates. One thing Amber and I know for certain: there is no way we would have Mercer had we not both been in a growing relationship with Christ, seeking His will for our lives together.

Paul said in Ephesians 1:5 (MSG), "Long, long ago he decided to adopt us into his family through Jesus Christ. (What pleasure he took in planning this!)" The beautiful picture of our taking Mercer home as our own and as a joint heir with Mars is exactly the way any of us come into a relationship with God through the sacrifice of Christ as joint heirs with Him—adoption.

The Gospel According to Barry Zito

The New Testament contains four different accounts of the gospel that all begin with the words: "The gospel according to. . . ." Then, of course, Paul's account of the gospel takes up several books. Once we encounter Christ for ourselves and enter into a relationship with Him, our own story begins. God then offers each of us an opportunity to present the gospel in our own way from our own unique perspective and personal history. The message is the same, but the method is as unique as He created us to be. That said, I want to explain what the gospel, or the good news of Jesus Christ, means to me personally and why He was my last stop in a long search for the truth through many religions and spiritual practices.

I must begin with one important fact about myself: I had almost *no* preconceived notions of Christians or Christianity when the gospel was presented to me. Growing up in an Eastern-type tradition, I was shielded from the hypocrisy and judgment that many experience in the churches of their youth. So many, particularly in the United States, have had the misfortune of interacting with someone along the way who misrepresented Christ's teachings. This situation always makes me so sad, and I do not take it lightly. If this has happened to you, I want to encourage you to not throw the baby out with the bathwater, so to speak. I encourage you to read my words with fresh eyes and an open heart, as if you had never heard any of it before. I was fortunate to hear what the gospel really is without being triggered by *anything* from my past. So once I heard the good news for the first time, my life was changed. My hope is that you might attempt to hear the message of Jesus in the same way I did. And we can all use a little good news every now and then, right?

First, we have to talk a bit about the bad news. As I have shared in this book, I thought I was a pretty good guy. I was trying hard to please whatever "god" I was chasing at the time. Yet *me* actually being the problem never crossed my mind. Here's what the apostle Paul said about my self-perceived goodness: "Everyone has sinned" (Rom. 3:23 NLT). Sounds kind of harsh, right? Well, if we don't know the actual meaning, sin can be an abrasive word and may even create an adverse reaction in us. It certainly did in me. If the word *sin* trips you up, you should know that the original word was an archery term, meaning literally to "miss the mark." If you missed the bull's-eye with your arrow, you sinned. You weren't *perfect*. We can likely all agree we aren't perfect, even on our best days. So if you read the passage again, you will see that it simply reminds us of the reality that we aren't perfect. When I heard this explanation, the truth of the statement resonated in me. Finally! Someone was telling me the truth about *me*, and I *knew* it was accurate from personal experience.

The second part of the passage is, "We all fall short of God's glorious standard," which begs the question, what *is* God's standard? If we are all missing the mark, then what is the mark that God wants us to hit anyway? Jesus said, "Be perfect, therefore, as your heavenly Father is perfect" (Matt. 5:48). So God expects perfection from us, a bull's-eye every time, which is not good because if we don't hit perfection, we won't ever get God's help with this really difficult thing called life on planet Earth.

So wait—if I am not perfect, then I can't have a relationship with a perfect God? Not fair! But that is the problem we all have. We must deal with the fact that God is just. The consequence of our actions with no exceptions is that we are born without a relational connection to God. If this problem isn't fixed, it will carry on into our eternity. God can't overlook even one small mistake without compromising His character. If He weren't a just God, then He would be something like a judge in a courtroom who lets a convicted mass murderer go free with no consequence for his actions. Our problem is that we each are the guilty party in this courtroom scene.

I will admit that I prefer a just God who enforces a consequence on others for their wrong actions *toward* me. But being totally honest with you, I would much rather God be a little easier when I mess up and let me off the hook by forgiving me. But I can't have this situation both ways, and neither can you. Nobody gets off the hook. If God is in fact a just God, then none of us deserve a relationship with Him and none of us can earn it.

There seems to be only two obvious solutions to this major problem. One being I have to figure out how to be perfect, or two, God has to lower His standard. But neither of these is actually possible. However, there is a third option where love prevails and God doesn't compromise. This third option is what the Bible is all about.

God's Word is really a love story about how He went about fixing this monumental problem that the first two humans created and we have carried on ever since. The story contained in Scripture was written over a 1,500-year span by about forty different authors, yet tells *one cohesive story* with incredible unity.

As I read the Bible for myself, I learned that God loves me more than I could fathom and He was not at all okay with my being separated from Him. Out of His immense love for us all, He came up with a solution: "For God so loved the world that he gave his one and only Son" (John 3:16). Jesus was sent to earth for one reason: to solve the problem of our separation from God.

Sin was so serious that the death of the God-man, Jesus, was required. God requires perfection. We can never deliver perfection. And as a result, there is a huge gap that must be filled. Being that Jesus never sinned and was perfect while He lived on earth, He could fill that gap. He paid the debt of perfection that we could never pay.

When Jesus was crucified and uttered the words, "It is finished," He took care of our past, present, and future sins. So even as sinful as we still are today, God only sees us as perfect and righteous, just as Jesus was and still is.

In the resurrection, when He rose from the grave three days later, He proved that He was in fact God and that His payment for sin worked. The most important thing to realize is that God loves us so much that He figured out a way to get us back after we had turned our backs on Him, all the while maintaining both His justice and love. Let's take that same sentence and personalize it for you: The most important thing to realize is that God loves *you* so much that He figured out a way to get *you* back after you turned your back on Him, all the while maintaining both His justice and love. This is the best story you will ever hear and it is true!

This message of grace, as well as an opportunity for a relationship with God that is unearned, flew in the face of what I had pursued my whole life. I was trying to fix myself and earn God's love through my baseball performance and pleasing people. I couldn't believe the freedom that came from realizing that I didn't need to *earn* any of God's love. It was a gift! This is what grace is, simply put, *unmerited favor*. Grace is how God relates to people. This concept not only changed my life, but I believe it can change the world, one heart at a time. When I am being honest with myself, crappy old me doesn't deserve the love of the most perfect Creator of the universe, but He gave it to me anyway.

The coolest part about grace is that He never forsakes me for screwing up. If He shamed me, I would surely turn my back on Him out of spite. But He never does, because our relationship is based on *grace*. I didn't earn it to start with, so I can't lose it by my lack of performance. God just says, "I know, Barry. You screwed up again, but I still love you. I still forgive you." His response inspires me to do a little better each time, because it doesn't feel good letting down Someone I love over and over and over.

I think of this like a marriage. If I came home and told my wife I had kissed a girl at a bar, and she instantly freaked out and kicked me out of the house, I would feel terrible. But not nearly as terrible as if she gave me a loving embrace and said, "Honey, there's nothing you can do that will change my love for you. I forgive you, and I will forgive you again if you do the same thing tomorrow." If she said that, I would literally crumble at her feet and do all I could to never disrespect her again. Behaving that way would take a big person, but the crazy part is that's what God does every time I tell Him I screwed up, whether it was gossiping about a friend or lusting after an image of a woman on the Internet. God lovingly takes me back, every time.

The God of the Bible is the only God in any religion who actually pursues people who do not deserve His love. Christianity is the only major world religion that is founded on the principle of grace. In every other spiritual practice I was involved in, it was up to me to go find God. And trust me, I tried. It was exhausting and I could never relax, because the search always required more effort. The beautiful thing about God is that He respected my free will so much that, even in all His power, He never forced me to come to Him. He waited patiently while I denied Him for many years as I pursued every selfish avenue I could find to get what I thought I needed: success, fame, possessions, women, human approval, and my dad's love. But eventually those were all dead-end roads and resulted only in more pain and emptiness in my heart. But even at that point, God didn't say, "See, Barry, I told you so!" He still just waited patiently. "So the LORD must wait for you to come to him so he can show you his love and compassion" (Isa. 30:18 NLT).

Hearing the message of Jesus and how much God loves me and desperately wanted me to make a decision to be His was a pivotal moment in my life. Since I could not un-hear the good news that I could come into a relationship with the God of the universe, I was forced to make a decision one way or another. Do I go on chasing my tail, relying on myself to put out all my own fires? Or do I admit that I can't do life alone anymore and fall into His loving arms that I have been searching for all my life?

For me, the decision was obvious. Worn out from a life of following my selfish will, I was ready. At that point, I prayed "the prayer," as they say. I professed that I believed the story was true. I believed that Jesus was God's perfect Son, and that He paid the debt for my sin that I never could, and arose from the dead. I happily admitted I had been falling short of God's perfect standard and apologized to Him. I told God I wanted a relationship with Him through Jesus. Ever since then He has been alive in my heart and working in my life. God has given me more peace than I could have ever imagined. And He's ready to do the same thing for you. All you need to do is believe.

"Are you tired? Worn out? Burned out on religion? Come to me.

Get away with me and you'll recover your life. I'll show you how to take a real rest. Walk with me and work with me—watch how I do it.

Learn the unforced rhythms of grace. I won't lay anything heavy or ill-fitting on you. Keep company with me and you'll learn to live freely and lightly." (Matt. 11:28–30, MSG)

Barry Zito Baseball Career Awards and Stats

Awards

COLLEGE:

Pac-10 Pitcher of the Year, 1999

First Team College All-American, 1999

Pac-10 Conference All-Star, 1999

MAJOR LEAGUE:

2001 Season

American League Player of the Week (September 4-10): awarded by Major League Baseball.

American League Pitcher of the Month (August): awarded by Baseball Writers and Broadcasters.

American League Pitcher of the Month (September).

2002 Season

Cy Young Award (American League)—honoring the best pitcher in Major League Baseball: awarded by the Baseball Writers' Association of America.

Players Choice Outstanding Pitcher of the Year Award (American League): awarded by members of the Major League Baseball Players Association. (Proceeds benefit the Players Trust for Children.)

American League All-Star Team: awarded by Major League Baseball.

Sporting News Pitcher of the Year Award: awarded by *Sporting News*, the most respected media outlet in baseball coverage.

2003 Season

Player of the Week Award (April 28–May 4, American League): awarded by Major League Baseball.

American League All-Star Team: awarded by Major League Baseball.

2005 Season

American League Pitcher of the Month (July): awarded by Baseball Writers and Broadcasters.

2006 Season

American League All-Star Team: awarded by Major League Baseball.

2010 Season

World Series Championship: awarded by Major League Baseball.

2012 Season

World Series Championship: awarded by Major League Baseball.

Hutch Award: created in 1965 in honor of the late pitcher/manager Fred Hutchinson, given to the player each season who best exemplifies Hutch's fighting spirit and competitive desire.

Lou Gehrig Memorial Award: created by Phi Delta Theta at Columbia University, Lou Gehrig's college fraternity, presented each season to the player who best exemplifies the character of Lou Gehrig, both on and off the field.

2015

Willie, Mickey and the Duke Award, shared with former A's teammates Tim Hudson and Mark Mulder (Trio of Aces): created in 1995 and presented each season by the New York Baseball Writers' Association to baseball personalities forever linked in sports history.

2017

National Italian American Sports Hall of Fame, class of 2017 inductee.

Major League Teams

Oakland Athletics: 2000–2006

San Francisco Giants: 2007–2013

Oakland Athletics: 2015

Major League Stats

Win-Loss: 165-143

ERA: 4.04

Strikeouts: 1,885

Games: 433

Games started: 421

Innings pitched: 2,576.2

WHIP: 1.34

Statistics By Year

	Team	IP	W/L	ERA
2000	A's	92.2	7-4	2.72
2001	A's	214.1	17-8	3.49
2002	A's	229.1	23-5	2.75
2003	A's	231.2	14-12	3.30
2004	A's	213.0	11-11	4.48
2005	A's	228.1	14-13	3.86
2006	A's	221.0	16-10	3.83
2007	Giants	196.2	11-13	4.53
2008	Giants	180.0	10-17	5.15
2009	Giants	192.0	10-13	4.03
2010	Giants	199.1	9-14	4.15
2011	Giants	53.2	3-4	5.87
2012	Giants	184.1	15-8	4.15
2013	Giants	133.1	5-11	5.74
2014	Inactive	-	-	-
2015	A's (AAA)	138.0	8-7	3.46
2015	A's	7.0	0-0	10.29

Notes

INTRODUCTION: FAME, SHAME, AND THE LOVE OF THE GAME

1. "If San Fran Wins the World Series Does Barry Zito Get a Ring?,"
   ProSportsDaily, October 20, 2010, accessed October 15, 2018,
   https://forums.prosportsdaily.com/showthread.php?544477-If-San
   -Fran-wins-the-World-Series-does-Barry-Zito-get-a-ring.

CHAPTER 1: HALF-ITALIAN, ALL-AMERICAN

1. Jack Curry, "A Pitcher Outside the Curve," *New York Times*,
   February 24, 2003, accessed October 24, 2018, https://www
   .nytimes.com/2003/02/24/sports/baseball-a-pitcher-outside-the
   -curve.html.

CHAPTER 2: LET THE GAMES BEGIN

1. Bruce Jenkins, "Barry Zito Is an Original—Just Like His Dad," *SF
   Gate*, June 21, 2013, accessed October 31, 2018, https://www
   .sfgate.com/sports/article/Barry-Zito-is-an-original-just-like-his
   -dad-4615908.php.

CHAPTER 3: THE POINT OF RELEASE IS EVERYTHING

1. Jenkins, "Barry Zito Is an Original—Just Like His Dad."

CHAPTER 4: METHOD TO THE MADNESS

1. Chris Jones, "He Came from Outer Space," *Esquire*, January 29,
   2007, accessed November 5, 2018, https://www.esquire.com/sports
   /a1221/barry-zito-profile-0602/.

CHAPTER 5: AT LEAST NOW WE'RE IN THE BUILDING

1. Lee Jenkins, "Zito's Father Played His Role to Perfection," *New York Times*, December 4, 2006, accessed November 8, 2018, https://www.nytimes.com/2006/12/04/sports/baseball/04zito.html.

CHAPTER 6: RIDE THAT WAVE

1. Michael Silver, "Inside the Head of Barry Zito as He Struggles to Regain His Cy Young Form, Oakland's Free-Spirited Lefty is Relying on His Best Stuff: Positive Thoughts and Faith in Himself," *Sports Illustrated*, June 21, 2004, accessed November 16, 2018, https://www.si.com/vault/2004/06/21/374474/inside-the-head -of-barry-zito-as-he-struggles-to-regain-his-cy-young-form -oaklands-free-spirited-lefty-is-relying-on-his-best-stuff-positive -thoughts-and-faith-in-himself.

CHAPTER 7: CREATING MY OWN MONSTER

1. Mitch Horowitz, "Barry's Way," *Science of Mind*, September 2003, accessed November 12, 2018, https://mitchhorowitz.com/other -writings/barrys-way/.
2. Tyler Kepner, "Baseball: Zito Beats Martinez to Win First Cy Young Award," *New York Times*, November 8, 2002, accessed November 12, 2018, https://www.nytimes.com/2002/11/08/sports/baseball -zito-beats-martinez-to-win-first-cy-young-award.html.

CHAPTER 8: TATTOO THAT NUMBER ON YOUR FOREHEAD

1. Silver, "Inside the Head of Barry Zito."
2. Silver, "Inside the Head of Barry Zito."
3. Silver, "Inside the Head of Barry Zito."

CHAPTER 9: TRYING EVERYTHING, GETTING NOWHERE

1. Pat Jordan, "The Mystery of Barry Zito," *New York Times*, September 12, 2008, accessed November 26, 2018, https://www.nytimes.com/2008/09/14/sports/playmagazine/0914play-ZITO.html.

CHAPTER 10: NOBODY'S FAULT BUT MINE

1. Lori Preuitt, "Zito Officially Benched," NBC Bay Area Sports, October 7, 2010, accessed November 26, 2018, https://www

.nbcbayarea.com/news/sports/Zito-Officially-Benched-104531804
.html.

CHAPTER 11: BUT HE WAS NEVER THERE, UNTIL RIGHT NOW

1. Tim Keown, "A Man in the Game," ESPN MLB, December 1, 2012, accessed November 30, 2018, http://www.espn.com/mlb/story/_/id /8682493/giants-pitcher-barry-zito-career-turnaround-amazing -season-espn-magazine-interview-issue.
2. Mental Health America, "Co-Dependency," accessed December 3, 2018, http://www.mentalhealthamerica.net/co-dependency.
3. Codependents Anonymous, "The Twelve Steps of Co-Dependents Anonymous," 2010, accessed December 3, 2018, http://coda.org /default/assets/File/Foundational%20Documents/Twelve%20Steps .pdf.

CHAPTER 12: STAY ON YOUR SIDE OF THE FENCE

1. Aaron M. Little and Shannon Woodland, "Former Baseball All-Star Finds New Identity off the Field," *The 700 Club*, accessed December 7, 2018, http://www1.cbn.com/former-baseball-all-star-finds-new -identity-field.
2. Fox Sports, "Giants' Sabean Hopes to Re-Sign Pence, Lincecum," September 28, 2013, accessed December 12, 2018, https://www .foxsports.com/mlb/story/giants-sabean-hopes-to-resign-pence -lincecum-05089352-092813.

CHAPTER 13: NO REGRETS, NO WHAT-IFS

1. Adam Berry, "Longtime Bay Area Pitcher Zito Officially Retires," MLB News, October 19, 2015, accessed December 14, 2018, https://www .mlb.com/news/athletics-giants-pitcher-barry-zito-retires/c-154937190.

About the Authors

Barry Zito is a Cy Young Award winner and two-time World Series champion who pitched primarily for the Oakland Athletics and San Francisco Giants throughout his Major League Baseball career. After retiring from baseball, Barry settled in Nashville, Tennessee, with his wife, Amber, and their two sons. Since 2015, he has been focused on his second career as a songwriter, musician, and author. His first album is titled *No Secrets*. Visit barryzitomusic.com.

Robert Noland has written more than seventy-five titles spanning across children, youth, and adult audiences over the past twenty-five years. He is an author, writer, editor, and project manager for Christian publishers, ministries, and faith-based organizations. He lives in Franklin, Tennessee, with his wife of thirty-plus years and has two adult sons. Visit robertnoland.com.